Heart Work

A Memoir

Heart Work

A Family Pilgrimage Inspired by Sibling Grief

Mary Jane Gandour

"Turning-Point," translation copyright © 1982 by Stephen Mitchell; from *Selected Poetry of Rainer Maria Rilke* by Rainer Maria Rilke, translated by Stephen Mitchell. Used by permission of Random House, an imprint and division of Penguin Random House LLC. All rights reserved.

Brief quotes from p. 89 and p. 91 in *Pilgrim Heart: The Inner Journey Home* by Sarah York, copyrighted © 2001 by Sarah York. Reprinted by permission of Sarah York.

"We Look with Uncertainty." All rights reserved. Printed by kind permission of the poet, Anne Hillman. *Awakening the Energies of Love*; *The Dancing of Animal Woman*, http://www.annehillman.net

Excerpt from *Letters to Young Poet* by Rainer Maria Rilke, translated by Stephen Mitchell, translation copyright © 1984 by Stephen Mitchell. Used by permission of Random House, an imprint and division of Penguin Random House LLC. All rights reserved.

Excerpt from *Cutting for Stone: A Novel* by Abraham Verghese, copyright © 2009 by Abraham Verghese. Used by permission of Alfred A. Knopf, an imprint of the Knopf Doubleday Publishing Group, a division of Penguin Random House LLC. All rights reserved.

Brief quote from Courtney E. Martin. "A Little Compartmentalization is a Life-Sustaining Thing." Blog post. *On Being* (onbeing.org). June 12, 2015. Used with permission.

Brief quote from pp. 16 & 26 from *Owning Your Own Shadow* by Robert A. Johnson. Copyrighted © 1991 by Robert A. Johnson. Reprinted by permission of HarperCollins Publishers.

Brief quote from p. 5 in *Learning to Walk in the Dark* by Barbara Brown Taylor. Copyrighted © 2014 by Barbara Brown Taylor. Reprinted by permission of HarperCollins Publishers.

Brief quote from *The Collected Works of C.G. Jung, Vol. 13: Alchemical Studies* by C.G. Jung and translated by R.F.C. Hull, Copyright © 1967 and 1995 by Princeton University Press. Reprinted by permission.

Brief quotes from p. 42 and pp. 96-97 in *Healing through the Dark Emotions* by Miriam Greenspan. Copyrighted © 2003 by Miriam Greenspan. Reprinted by permission of Shambhala Publications.

Brief quote from pp. 15-16 in *Consolations* by David Whyte. Copyrighted © 2014 by David Whyte. Reprinted by permission of Many Rivers Press, Langley, WA.

Copyright © 2016 by Mary Jane Gandour
All rights reserved

ISBN-13: 978-1539311645
ISBN-10: 1539311643
Printed by CreateSpace, an Amazon.com Company
Available from Amazon.com and other retail outlets.

For Molly

Work of the eyes is done, now

go and do heart-work

on all the images imprisoned within you

Rainer Maria Rilke

CONTENTS

Prologue   1

CHAPTER ONE ~ ***Venturing into the Unknown***   5

CHAPTER TWO ~ ***Gathering in the Heartland***   11

CHAPTER THREE ~ ***Wandering in the Wilderness***   29

    Interviews on cell phones   30

    Diaries on a bottom shelf   38

    Medical issues in an accordion file   93

    Christmas boxes in the garage   109

CHAPTER FOUR ~ ***Returning with the Questions***   117

    Death Talk   119

    Normalcy and Compartmentalization   126

    From Shadow to Light   131

    Relationships in our Family   137

Epilogue   145

Gratitudes   149

Notes   151

Appendices   155

"I Remember"   173

Prologue

Infrequently in our human journey, life-changing days come along with their moment of redefinition and a clearly drawn line between past and future. After we cross that line, life will never be the same, even though we don't comprehend that reality at the time. Only later do we realize the discontinuity and begin to grasp the rupture that redefined time from that day forward.

I remember the waiting room in Hematology Clinic B at Riley Hospital for Children in Indianapolis, Indiana, on January 22, 1986, the day our six-year-old Aimee was diagnosed with Acute Lymphoblastic Leukemia. Her face, framed on each side by long, dark brown braids, was expressionless as she sat there in her yellow jogging outfit with its pink bear appliqué. The room was quiet and filled with rows of solemn-looking parents and their children who looked quite ill to us. Our two-year-old Molly began banging pots and pans together in the play area kitchen as my husband Jack, Aimee and I headed back to an exam room for a bone marrow aspiration, the ultimate diagnostic procedure and predictor of treatment's course. I smelled chemicals, drugs as yet unnamed and unidentified, drugs yet to enter my daughter's body.

When we returned with a diagnosis, Molly had already made friends with a nurse she called "the purple lady" who was pretending to eat some of this toddler's imaginary cooking creations. Ten days later Molly helped to push her weakened sister's wheelchair down the hallway from her hospital room toward the elevator, the beginning of our hour and a half trip home to West Lafayette. We had already initiated what would become longstanding relationships with cancer professionals and a disease that ultimately refused to do their bidding.

On March 26, 1994, eight years and two months after this diagnosis, our family as we knew it disappeared when Aimee died around sunset. It took years to inhale rather than gasp that truth, and many more years to open our mouths in an undefended, vulnerable way to discuss our loss as a family. By then Molly had grown into adulthood. She had become a filmmaker and was living in Brooklyn, New York. In her mid-twenties she began to stir up grief that I thought had been integrated into our lives. But, as we were to discover, that had not been the case for her. So sixteen years after Aimee's death, at Molly's request, we began the therapeutic work I describe herein from my perspective. It's a status report really, for our lifelong grief journey continues to evolve in ways we could not have predicted, both for Molly as a sibling and all of us as a family.

I don't believe this particular story has been written before, certainly not with this level of detail and from a mother's point of view. My reaction to the depth of our therapeutic venture and the intensity of my stirred-up feelings was to write and keep writing, also to educate myself by reading, but to continue documenting, expressing, writing.

Even though the word *journey* kept appearing in what I wrote, I had no idea that we had taken the first steps of a pilgrimage. When our therapist used the term *heart pilgrimage*, its full meaning was lost on me. I was equally unable to characterize what we were doing as *heart work* even though it had more to do with feelings than intellect and required serious labor. Only as I consistently took up my pen or touched my keyboard or searched for reading resources did I begin to understand what we were doing at a metaphorical level.

So many elements of pilgrimage were present in our story: leaving the routines of everyday life, moving to new vantage points, walking on the ground of sacred events, experiencing confusion and disorientation, confronting fears and struggles, returning with new awareness, wanting to stay in this place of growth. Our journey involved traveling with our hearts rather than to a defined destination. Our work together surely qualified as a pilgrimage.

Sarah York's book *Pilgrim Heart: The Inner Journey Home* was enormously helpful to me as I conceptualized about our experience. Her description of pilgrimage, which involved Separation, Crossing the Threshold, Transformation, and Reincorporation, fit beautifully with what our family had experienced.[1] These four descriptors helped to organize the chapters of this book. I changed their wording to more accurately express our particular story.

Separation is initiated when the pilgrim plans to leave the known for the unknown and begins to make preparations. For us, this was Molly's invitation, years after Aimee's death, to leave the familiar for deeper and riskier work exploring our experiences with her sister's life, illness and death, and with each other. We accepted her invitation. **Venturing into the Unknown** describes the early planning and evolution of this journey.

In Crossing the Threshold the pilgrim moves from the ordinary to the sacred where the everyday structures of life get turned upside down. For us, this time involved six weeks of intensive therapy, interviews, conversations, re-visiting the hospital, looking at scrapbooks. It also included less structured time over Christmas later that year. These shared experiences took us out of our comfort zones, often to issues we had not planned to visit. **Gathering in the Heartland** describes this arduous process, the groundwork that made growth possible.

Transformation is spent in the mysterious wilderness struggling with fears and confronting inner conflict. Uncomfortable feelings surrounded my questions for Molly after therapy, the unread diaries sitting on my bookshelf, her questions for me about Aimee's medical treatment, and issues involving Christmas over the years. **Wandering in the Wilderness** describes the longest, most confusing, and most fruitful phase of pilgrimage for me. Not surprisingly, it is the lengthiest chapter in this book. It contains a story within the larger story in its subchapter, *Diaries on the Bottom Shelf*, important reading for understanding the background of our journey.

Reincorporation involves returning to former situations and roles to examine how they are different, how the pilgrim is different. I found myself unable and unwilling to fully resume my former way of being. I was exploring new ways to relate to my family and to be more authentically myself. **Returning with the Questions** describes the challenge of living with unanswered questions while simultaneously nurturing the energy and comfort of the pilgrimage.

At the beginning of each chapter and subchapter, there are italicized *reflections*—writings by our daughters, journal entries of mine, quotations or poems—to ease the way into the subject matter that follows. I included them because they are meaningful to me and expressive of something about one of us, our family, or the themes of pilgrimage. Poems or quotations by others are used with the permission of their publishers. They are listed on the copyright page in their order of appearance in the text.

At the end of the book are *Appendices*. The first two are timelines for orientation to our family's grief work and the history of Aimee's disease. The other appendices can be read in tandem with the text to expand it—or later as a way to transition out of the book.

Initially I did this therapeutic work for Molly; I never considered not doing it. I love her deeply and wanted to help her further relearn life without her sister. I did it for Aimee, also deeply loved, to know her better and to re-examine the gift of her life. I did it for my family, the growth and understanding of all of us in the aftermath of this shattering loss. Ultimately I recognized that I had done it for myself as well, without acknowledging or understanding this truth at the beginning.

The desire to write about our experience came from deep inside me, a beckoning so powerful that I simply accepted it. Molly's return to Indiana to work on her sibling grief inspired our family pilgrimage. In writing about it from my point of view, I came to understand the story better and to learn more about who I was and am in it.

I am a psychologist by training, but on these pages I am a mother telling her story. To write these words is part of my healing as a human being and grieving mother.

Chapter One ~*Venturing into the Unknown*

Simple Things

Old chewed-up tennis shoes,
Staying up at night till two,
Playing dress-up with Mom's old clothes,
Running outside after the first big snow,
Loose, lazy summer days,
Making wild flower bouquets,
Worn teddy bears you've had since one,
The championship game that our team won,
Stuffing yourself on Thanksgiving Day,
At recess, finally going out to play,
Ice cream served in a humungous dish,
A four-leaf clover on which to make a wish,
Burnt, black marshmallows that we had on s'mores,
The last day of school when you run out the doors.

Simple though these fun things may be,
Together they mean happiness for me.
So if there's a sorrow you want to surmount,
Remember, in life, it's the little things that count.

>Molly Gandour
>January, 1995
>Ten months after her sister's death

My grief rekindled unexpectedly in 2009 with a request from our then twenty-six-year-old filmmaker daughter, Molly. She had flown home for a weekend visit to Indiana, an autumn escape from the intensity of the New York City life she found so stimulating.[1] On the drive home from the Indianapolis airport to West Lafayette, Molly mentioned that she wanted to talk with us about something while she was home. My husband Jack and I later admitted to each other that our minds had run a gamut of topics. Grief hadn't been on either of our lists.

"I would really like for our family to do some creative project related to Aimee's death," came the topic in the midst of other chatter two nights later, after finishing dinner and moving to another room. Molly went on to say that she thought we had a lot more work to do as a family on her older sister's death. She'd been talking to a therapist about this, turning over various possibilities in her mind, feeling this need very powerfully.

"I think that prospect is really exciting, Molly. It's odd because I've had some similar thoughts lately, pretty vague thoughts with no real direction. It sounds like you have ideas that are much more spelled out," I responded.

I flashed back to my stock answer for inquiries about how ten-year-old Molly was doing after her fourteen-year-old sister Aimee's death of leukemia in 1994. "She seems to be doing ok, but she'll probably need a lot of therapy when she's, say, around twenty-four," I'd respond, sometimes with a bit of a smile. End of inquiry. People rarely wanted specifics. I'd pulled that age out of my storehouse of educated guesses, but it turned out not to be far from the truth.

I was surprised by Molly's request—intrigued, excited and quietly relieved. I had for years sensed that there was much more to her grief process than we understood. Here she sat articulating a proposal that could only come from her. Jack and I only had to look at each other to know we were both onboard. Even though her ideas weren't fully formulated yet, she was suggesting hours of interaction among the three of us, going to family therapy, possibly filming all of it. Exactly how we could arrange this time together, when and where, under what circumstances, was not clear. Molly asked for our assistance in further defining these plans and figuring out how we could make them happen. At that moment, her proposal became a family project.

We didn't fully embark on this journey until six months later, but from that October day forward, my relationship with Molly and our family dynamics have never been the same.

The autumn continued to manifest its usual Indiana glory, gradually replaced by grey skies and bare trees, followed by extreme cold and frequent snow fall. As we did intermittent planning over these months, I found myself thinking about the years after Aimee's death with increasing frequency and intensity. This anticipatory time became a private retreat for me, as I once again revisited familiar territory in my mind and heart.

I remembered weeping and holding my dead daughter's body before the three of us finally left the hospital in a daze. We created a funeral that expressed and honored Aimee as fully as we could with music, dance, words, and her friends as pall bearers. Molly helped to choose the music, played *Amazing Grace* on the piano, and stood in the receiving line with us. Jack gave the eulogy. Grandparents, aunts, uncles, cousins, friends and our community surrounded us with their love and bereavement.

Aimee died on Passover, and Easter arrived the following weekend. I remembered a small tree beautifully decorated with Lithuanian painted eggs arriving from Molly's class soon after the funeral. The next weekend Easter lilies from some of Aimee's friends adorned our front steps. Daffodils were blossoming everywhere.

I pictured myself returning medical equipment, disposing of medications, writing hundreds of thank you notes, smelling Aimee's sheets and clothes, listening to Benedictine chants, reading the daily batch of sympathy cards and notes, and visiting the cemetery every day. I avoided the church where Aimee's funeral was held, the school she attended, the hospital where she died, sometimes even her friends and their parents who were my friends.

For months I felt exhausted and had a difficult time keeping myself awake in the evening. I couldn't write anything about what I was going through or read any of the books friends had so kindly given us. There was a layer of gauze around me, grief gauze, which shaped my view of the world and filtered what impinged upon my senses.

I recalled Molly crying at bedtime as she tried to settle into sleep. Hugging her, I cried with her. She wore her sister's clothes, sat at Aimee's desk to do her homework, and wrote daily entries in her Dear Aimee diary with its blue sky, white clouds cover. Her friends asked if she was going to move into her sister's larger bedroom. Molly answered that she wasn't ready for that yet. Based upon what I read in articles, learned at workshops, heard from her teacher, and intuited as a mother, I thought that Molly was grieving quite appropriately for a ten-year-old.

Heart Work

I recollected how work grounded and comforted me when I returned to my psychotherapy office a month after the funeral. I felt a sense of competence. I had always loved the science, art and privilege of working with people in therapy. For all the uncertainties of what any given day might bring, work felt secure to me as long as I never had to see a child with cancer. The routine was familiar. My office felt like a refuge. Molly went to school. Jack and I went to work. Routine brought some comfort to us.

But I also remembered that routine didn't really feel like routine without Aimee. She wasn't beside Molly in the back seat of our dark green van. She wasn't sitting at the kitchen table eating Cream of Wheat with red raspberries on top, her breakfast of choice in the months before she died. There weren't decisions about who was going to practice piano first. She didn't accompany us out to our old neighborhood for Monday afternoon piano lessons. She wasn't in the crafts room or the family room. Jack and the girls' Thursday trips to the grocery store, which had gone on for years, were reduced to a dyad whose roles became blurred without Aimee's clearly defined presence in that enterprise. There were only three places at the dinner table and fewer hands for the clean-up afterwards. She wasn't there for "good nights" or getting ready for school in the morning. The house felt quiet and lonely to all of us.

I thought of our family taking flowers and wreaths to the cemetery, going to Mass on anniversary dates, lighting a candle for Aimee at dinner on every major holiday, and planting an October Glory maple tree for her in the middle of our backyard.

I reminisced about attending a memorial for Aimee at the hospital chapel where Molly and I passed out programs and materials about her sister to her medical caretakers. I recalled the entire day of rituals for our family and friends on the one-year anniversary of Aimee's death. There were awards in Aimee's name at the junior/senior high school. Molly had won one of them. I remembered attending the graduation ceremony and parties of the Class of 1998, Aimee's class.

I felt my unease from years ago when grief resources extended to Molly never fully took hold. The grade school counselor's open door policy for her, not accessed beyond the scheduled meetings soon after

Aimee's death. The children's loss group that she signed up for, later cancelled for lack of participants. Molly's rejection of her high school counselor's invitation to join an ongoing grief group that had been started for Aimee's friends, who by then were in college.

I remembered my brother Ed's advice, "You need to create a history for yourselves as a threesome," which we fully embraced. We started annual vacation trips the summer after Aimee's death. We covered massive expanses of this country over the years, guided by carefully crafted itineraries devised by Jack. National parks far and wide, bodies of water on every side of this country, cities large and small, seats of government, scenes of battles, lakes and rivers, mountains and plains, towers and craters. We drove and drove.

In later years, there were trips to England, China and Thailand, work related for Jack, but occasions for us to travel, experience, and create more shared history.

I thought about our annual autumn trips to Keeneland Racecourse in Lexington, Kentucky. At face value, they were a chance to get together with extended family to enjoy the gorgeous horse country and bet on horse races. Beneath the surface, we were creating new family rituals and providing a predictable time for Molly to spend time with her cousin Rochelle who was Aimee's age.

I reminisced about our four birthdays, all in a row toward the end of the year: September - Jack, October - Molly, November - Aimee, December - Mary Jane. They spanned from the last heat of summer to the first snow of winter. After Aimee died, we continued to celebrate but with a diminished planning committee and the yearly challenge of observing her birthday in a meaningful way. Molly was confused and indecisive about her own birthday parties, particularly her 11th, just months after her sister's death, and later her 16th and 18th, both milestone birthdays that her sister never got to celebrate.

I remembered the loneliness and frustration I felt at Christmas dinners over the years when Aimee's absence was so apparent but not as fully recognized as I would have liked. I wondered why I was the one to carry the responsibility of keeping her memory alive every holiday season but was too afraid of what might happen if I didn't.

Heart Work

My remembrance retreat faded into the background in the early months of 2010 with the escalation of family deliberations about how to arrange our therapeutic work. There were phone calls and emails back and forth with a fairly measured, non-frenzied quality to them. We openly admitted to each other that this commitment felt like a real risk, but we continued working together to make it happen. Decisions were made. We'd get together in Indiana, not New York, during a time when Molly could fulfill her work obligations from a remote site, probably in the spring. Six weeks was the longest she could be away. Molly said that she did want to do some filming, and we consented to give it a try. The therapist we wanted to work with agreed to see us on the condition that she herself would not be filmed. We were to be in touch with her as soon as we had a time frame. Camera equipment transport was a major issue since Molly lived over a thousand miles away and didn't have a car. The equipment was too sensitive and bulky for airline travel. The train seemed like a possibility. The logistics were coming together.

I felt energized by our first round of plans and sensed that it would carry us along. I was curious about my daughter, sibling grief, my family, myself—hoping for some new slant on each of these topics in the weeks and months ahead. My strong impression was that we were about to enter unknown territory in our relationships and our history together.

Chapter Two ~ *Gathering in the Heartland*

April 12, 2010

Energy seems to be shifting as we anticipate Molly's arrival and the beginning of our work together. In my restlessness yesterday, I decided to clean up the crafts room in the basement—a trip into Aimee and Molly's shared world there. I chose to do this task in contrast to my usual avoidance of this space.

I folded up scraps of fabric, threw out dried up markers and bottles of acrylic paint, rearranged those that were still useable, put pipe cleaners back into cellophane packages and grouped together all the glue guns we had acquired over the years. I appreciated the little plastic containers Aimee had labeled and marveled at the variety of crafts the girls had done here together. Aimee was the older one, the leader, the more accomplished crafter, with four years of experience on her little sister. Molly nonetheless had been by her sister's side as they worked in their bubble of intensity, creativity and connectedness.

Molly didn't do as much in this room after Aimee died. Her time here involved groups of friends and specific projects like decorating sunglasses for a Hollywood birthday party or making costumes and props for a newly choreographed dance routine. The crafts room became a place where kids could gather and be messy in the basement of the Gandour house, a room with an oval hooked rug on a cement floor, exposed rafters, a washer and dryer at one end, and several bare light bulbs illuminating the place. There was an appeal to its tackiness.

By the time the three of us assembled, the sub-zero temperatures had given way to muddy puddles of melted snow. Daffodils were poking through the soil, and soon there were magnolia blossoms on the tree outside the window of Aimee's bedroom that long ago had become Molly's bedroom.

Heart Work

On a weekend in mid-April 2010, the Amtrak Cardinal train wended its way toward Indiana carrying Molly and her bundles of camera equipment. This twenty-four-hour journey started at Penn Station in New York and went through Philadelphia, Washington, D.C., Charleston, Cincinnati, Indianapolis, and finally to Lafayette where a dear family friend was waiting for Molly with coffee and a muffin in hand and enough space for the camera equipment in her car.

The following day Jack and I drove home from a weekend in Lexington, Kentucky, planned nearly a year before. We probably came close to some of the tracks Molly's train had traveled upon the day before. Our trip had given us a sense of new life—blossoming crabapple trees enhancing the landscape of Keeneland Racecourse, freshly painted horse farm fences, the scent of sprouting Kentucky bluegrass. After a day for Molly to settle in at home, we arrived to begin our family time together, yet to be fully planned out and certainly yet to be called a pilgrimage.

While unpacking, I began to feel the unique luxury of this situation. Parents could never ask an adult child to take six weeks out of her life and travel home to explore a loss that each family member was grieving deeply and uniquely. In the years following Aimee's death, the three of us had not sat down together for a sustained period of time to talk in depth about this tremendous loss, what we were feeling, how it was affecting us, how we were coping over time, how we were doing as a family, and where Aimee fit into our family and lives. There had been discussions between twosomes but not all three of us. No, parents could not ask a son or daughter for this gift, but an adult child could propose giving it, and they could dig deep inside themselves to wholeheartedly accept it.

We had a planning meeting that first Sunday night with Molly as the facilitator—a very professional, well-grounded woman who knew what she was doing technically and artistically. She was organized, informative, focused. We had already decided upon and arranged therapy twice a week, an hour and a half each session, mostly for the whole family but sometimes for Molly with her father or Molly with me. We also added one-hour interviews at home five days a week which would involve Molly interviewing each of us, one of us interviewing her, or Jack and I talking to each other. She planned to film each of these segments as well as our dinners at the dining room table. We also arranged a 'field trip' to the Indiana University Medical Center to seek out places we remembered from Aimee's treatment. We signed up for a clay and poetry workshop with an art therapist in Indianapolis. In between these activities, Molly planned to investigate the multiple bins of Aimee's artwork, school papers and mementos stacked up in the garage. On the weekends, we'd explore the broad shelf of Aimee's scrapbooks and another of Molly's. Each of us admitted to being nervous. We had little idea how this plan would work out.

Suddenly furniture was rearranged or slanted in new directions. Lamps were repositioned and pointed in unusual ways. Extra lights from various parts of the house, twisted at odd angles, appeared in the living and dining rooms. A large piece of foam board was available as an on-call backdrop. Blue masking tape markers appeared on the floor and the sides of cabinets. Two tripods with attached cameras became fixtures in our home although their locations shifted with the day, time and task. We became friends with their fuzzy, gray microphone covers and blinking red lights. The most consistent and uncompromising ritual of filming was "mic-ing up"—making sure our microphones were attached correctly and turned on. Nothing was filmed without mic-ing up.

With some initial awkwardness, we settled into our first filmed dinner, quickly forgetting about the technology accompanying us and finding ourselves absorbed in an attempt to combine our memories of that January 1986 day when Aimee was diagnosed.

The next evening my self-examination started immediately when I interviewed Molly for the first time. As I listened to her, I grasped that my daughter, the bereaved sibling, was revealing her own point of view for the first time, one that differed significantly from my own. I always knew that another perspective had to be there, but I had not heard Molly express much of it. Interwoven with some early recollections of her sister, Molly told me that Aimee's opinion had always mattered far more to her than her parents' point of view and that virtually every relationship in her life had been influenced profoundly by the loss of her sister. Her perspective was simply stated, briefly articulated, and deeply revelatory to me. I was shaken by these statements and suspected I would be hearing more.

The following morning, we started family therapy. Transporting two cameras and tripods as well as microphones to our therapist's office, getting them set up before our session, and packing them up afterwards were Molly's responsibilities. We saw family therapy as a way of coming together to explore our family grief, with our trusted therapist and each other as witnesses.

Molly said she wanted to reconnect with memories and how they affected each of us. She was seeking perspective. She explained that using film as a medium gave her more momentum and made her more accountable to whatever it documented. She was not trying to film anything in particular and wasn't sure if or how she would use this footage in the future. My sense was that the cameras gave Molly a structure and framework to ballast her journey into territory that was painful and uncharted for her. As silent witnesses, they became easy to ignore. Over the weeks, they came to feel like the presence of a powerful but silent older sister.

Our first therapy session was supposed to be organizational but ended up being a full-blown, fully filmed session. We had pushed two striped couches into an L-shape so that we could be closer to each other and accommodate the cameras better. We were off and running almost without realizing it in the soft colors and dim lights of this office. Once again we were surprised by how little we thought about film procedures as we settled into talking with each other.

"I feel so vulnerable doing this work with you," Molly stated in a shaky voice, avoiding all eye contact as she spoke these words. I couldn't understand why she felt so fearful about talking to us, but began to realize that she had feelings that were so deep, so much a part of her, and so alien to us. There were touching moments as we reminisced about our family and Aimee, but the most striking words were Molly's declarations—again that Aimee's death had profoundly affected every relationship in her life since then, and that as she was growing up, it seemed to her that nothing was really important unless it was life threatening.

I sensed a depth and complexity to her grief that ironically created unease in me after all my years of curiosity about her interior life related to her sister's illness and death.

Molly became a new person for me to know.

Our first week together became the most communicative time I could remember since we had become a threesome. We all took risks with self-disclosure. The range of emotions expressed was broad and variable. We were edgy and annoyed as well as affectionate and appreciative. We all cried, individually and together. Most dramatically, by the end of the week we all knew that being together included Aimee. It was about the four of us.

The week felt monumental to me.

Molly was unwavering in her commitment to the work as we had planned it. The interviews, dinners together, and therapy sessions continued on schedule. I was exhausted every night and processed only a fraction of what had happened because so much was happening. Even though I had cut back my work schedule for these weeks, I lacked the time and energy to journal about what had occurred each day. I also had a difficult time recalling our exact dialogue.

Over the weekend my mood shifted as the emotional drain of the first week started to sink in. I grasped that we had begun a major upheaval of how we had been walking together for years. I felt both exhilaration at the week's candid communication and skepticism about how we could possibly keep this up for five more weeks. The defensive part of me wanted to ask Molly all the predictable questions: Don't you know how much we love you, how hard we tried? Don't you know that we did the best we could under the circumstances? Don't you know that we were grieving deeply too? Don't you know how well you seemed to be grieving as a child? I strongly sensed that each of these questions would interfere with Molly's articulation of what she was trying to express. I stared down my defensiveness and softened around these questions. I made a solid decision to continue listening and learning, not sure of what I'd hear or what it might mean for our lives.

Heart Work

I became conscious of a terrified feeling inside me that had returned from Molly's adolescent years. I think it stemmed from an unconscious fear I had—that if I ever got into a full blown conflict with her, she would leave me too, and I would be *daughterless*—even though Molly had never in any way threatened this or done anything to make me think such rejection was possible. I knew that my fear of abandonment also had to go if I were to honestly engage in the inevitable conflict that would come along somewhere in this process.

What else would I have to give up, or at least soften around, to really hear Molly? Certainly my strongly held beliefs that I was an excellent mother to her through all these years, that I had always provided her with open communication whenever she needed it, that I accurately perceived her needs and acted in meaningful ways to meet them, that we were very close, that I was a role model for her, and, most importantly, the comforting idea that she was fine, just fine.

I can't explain how the shift out of those weekend feelings occurred, perhaps grace or providence, but it did. I do know that I became conscious of my own vulnerability, the price I would have to pay for enhanced authenticity. The sense that I needed to dig very deeply into myself and take substantial risks in my communication was powerful. I absorbed at a visceral level that Molly would not abandon me. I began to grasp how much I had to learn about her, our family, and certainly myself. I wanted to listen to all Molly had to say with curiosity and an open heart, even though I sometimes felt like she was talking to someone else, not me.

This shift of consciousness accompanied me into the second week, creating a new vantage point that supported and sustained me across the weeks ahead. I sensed reorganization inside myself, unplanned and unlabeled. Something involuntary and challenging but also stimulating. We had already begun exploring our loss of Aimee from Molly's perspective, and I knew that none of us would desert the treasured work we had begun. There was no turning back.

At the end of our third week, Molly and I spent a day at the Indiana University Medical Center in Indianapolis. We wanted to revisit the places where Aimee had been diagnosed, where her outpatient and inpatient treatment had taken place, and where she had died. Tracking down these locations involved visiting two different hospitals. In the course of the morning, we learned that some memorable places for us no longer existed in the same spots. The former location of Hematology Clinic B had become a patient library. The Pediatric Intensive Care Unit (PICU) had been converted into research labs. The ice cream shop with flavors named after James Whitcomb Riley's poems had been replaced by a McDonald's. We didn't see anyone we recognized. A receptionist asked me if I was in marketing. Later a volunteer wanted to know if I was a physician. Only one nurse we talked to remembered Aimee's hematologist. Both the connection and the disconnection we felt were disorienting for Molly and me.

Eventually we got hungry and happened to be in the hospital where Aimee had been treated during the last years of her life. We made the familiar first-floor walk past the chapel and gift shop, and then continued toward the cafeteria, wondering if it was still there. It was. As Molly and I entered, we were immediately confronted by an area of nearly total stainless steel where people lined up, took trays and silverware. Literally nothing had changed about it, nothing, not even the smell. The cereal boxes were in the same place as well as the milk cartons, the ice cream machine, the salad bar. I got light-headed and felt dizzy. I could feel my entire chest swelling with sadness and fear, my throat closing. I walked through this area as quickly as possible because I was unable to stop.

I spotted a sign for an Au Bon Pain tucked into the left side of the cafeteria, a new space with no old hospital associations for us. We headed in that direction, explored the options, and each selected something to eat. I had told Molly earlier that I'd pay for lunch but was having difficulty acting upon that self-assigned task. I stood there immobilized and staring at wrapped salads and sandwiches on a refrigerated shelf in front of me. My hand was touching my wallet inside my purse. Frozen. Silent.

"Mom, what is wrong with you? We have to pay."

In slow motion I took out my wallet, slid out my credit card and gave it to the cashier. I was annoyed by the abruptness and tone of

Molly's words. We walked outside and sat at a table in a nearby courtyard. I didn't express my irritation to Molly; I was too confused and drained to attempt it. Her face was inexpressive, and she also made no effort to process what had just happened. We talked about the tulips blooming nearby and how we'd spend the rest of the afternoon.

It would take a year, a lot more openness on both of our parts, and an opportune situation for me to understand what had actually happened during this cafeteria episode.

As we moved into the second half of our six weeks together, Molly held on to some of her black and white judgments about us. I was unable to access my anger about Aimee's death. Jack was more comfortable discussing facts than emotions. At the same time, the prevailing sense for us and our therapist was that we were three adults who cared very deeply about each other and Aimee. We touched on highly sensitive issues during these later weeks. My not wanting Molly to grow up. Aimee's 'canonization' after her death. The confusion of roles and relationships in our family without Aimee. A disagreement Jack and I had after attending an award in Aimee's name. Molly's feelings that she could never measure up to her sister or express negativity to her family. My wish to always have things nice. Our family not discussing Aimee's death together before it happened. Molly's loneliness for her sister during our yearly summer trips as a threesome. Her perception of Aimee as a more adept ambassador to Jack and me than she could ever be.

During our therapy sessions, there were warm hugs, sad faces, laughter, furrowed brows, tears, pauses, smiles, resistance, tenderness, and the quick passage of time. I didn't always know what words would come out of my mouth when I opened it. At times I could see the softening in both Jack and Molly, and I sensed it in myself.

Concurrently our interviews and dinner conversations continued at home. Sometimes the interviews were focused on information such as questions about Aimee's form of leukemia or particular drugs in her treatment regimen. At other times they were highly emotional, tearful renderings, question by question, of what a particular phase of treatment was like. Sometimes the same topic evoked differing levels of emotional intensity depending upon our moods and the context. At dinner, food often sat in front of the person talking the most, getting cold, later eaten in the same way we ate food at the hospital—just to sustain ourselves.

Over time I realized how little Molly knew and remembered about her sister's disease. I began to comprehend that her therapy issues had much more to do with the childhood emotional experience of loving her older sister and then watching her fade away and die, followed by the emotional pain and adjustment of living without Aimee during adolescence and young adulthood. It was this relationship that was Molly's primary concern as well as how her loss, our loss, influenced her relationships with Jack and me.

One of the ways Molly reconnected with her sister during this time at home was to sort through large plastic bins stuffed with selected school papers, art projects, drawings and notebooks from Aimee's preschool to eighth grade years. During the last week, Molly pulled out a four-foot-long tracing on butcher paper of Aimee's body colored with energized crayon strokes of green, red, orange and yellow with a shock of long, thick hair colored black and brown. Preschool, pre-cancer Aimee vibrantly expressing herself about herself. Molly showed it to us and said that we needed to hang it up somewhere. I had a same-scale colored copy of this Aimee image made and hung it in our crafts room where the girls had spent so much time together.

The next day, Molly invited us to sit at the dining room table where she had small slips of paper in a bowl with pens nearby and another larger empty bowl. She invited us to join her in sharing what stimulated memories of Aimee for us by randomly saying something out loud, writing it down on a slip of paper, folding it in half, and then placing it in the larger bowl. We sat for a long time, our voices clear and unhesitating. The litany went on, everything from Thai food to the musical *Annie* to Mammoth Cave in Kentucky, Care Bears, *Runaway Train,* Mother Goose nursery rhymes, Halloween. As time went on, the memory papers took up more volume and significance than the blank slips of paper. Eventually we tired and felt emotionally overloaded. It was time to stop for then. For everything we spoke and then wrote, there

Heart Work

was a story, links that could be clicked open for deeper levels of narrative and feeling.

Two days later, I sorted through all the reminders of Aimee we had written down. The memories were sweet. Various categories for them easily formulated in my mind, and I did some frequency counts. My not-very-scientific analysis indicated that what stimulated the most memories of Aimee were places in our home and around this town as well as crafts she had done and people who had supported her. Quite far down the list of category frequencies was the medical, indicating to me that our memories had more to do with Aimee's connectedness and expressiveness than her suffering. I found that realization comforting.

At the end of the week when she was about to return to New York, Molly presented us with a piece of art work that she had created the night before. It was an elegantly simple black and white drawing—a square house with a slanted roof and four rooms visible, each with a name artfully scripted inside: Mary Jane and Jack each in an upstairs room, Aimee and Molly each in a downstairs room. Our family together under one roof, each of us with equal share and representation. There was a child quality to its rendering and a sense of after-school paper presentation in its giving. Its symbolism, however, was very adult. Jack and I were thrilled. We also hung it in the crafts room as a symbolic representation of our six weeks together.

After a very emotional farewell, Molly and her camera equipment headed back to Brooklyn in a rental car. It would take time to absorb all that had happened and shifted within each of us. The redefined presence of all four of us in our family would take some settling into. Each of us held onto the belief that we would maintain and sustain our growth together.

"Being at home cracked open the whole world for me," was Molly's comment to us when she called to say she had arrived safely back in New York.

As the weeks and months went by, we all came to know that life *had* changed. Jack and I regularly revisited our family's therapeutic work—mostly during dinner conversations that expanded our insights. I felt a compulsion to talk about our experience with close friends and our relatives; they seemed genuinely interested. Molly said that her friends were incredulous and wished all of us well. She told one friend that she feared these changes would all disappear in the autumn, but they didn't. She said that her perspective on life had changed, adding, "It's huge. There's no going back, for any of us." I felt shifts in myself without any of the detailed lists and prescribed steps that normally accompanied my efforts at change. I embraced the path my family was walking together, hoping that reorientation and healing would continue to be part of it.

Themes and realizations had emerged. The tremendous importance of Aimee in each of our lives and the true depth of our loss. How much and how little Molly had perceived and remembered from childhood, and our inaccurate assumptions about this issue. How little we knew about each other's experience with Aimee's illness. Our difficulties with fully and honestly expressing our grief to Molly. How disadvantaged and yet protected she was by her young age when Aimee was alive. The moods, emotions and questions we tried to hide from each other.

We knew that we had more work to do, but its form was not clear to any of us. How much would we do together and individually? Molly wanted to eventually look at the footage she had shot. I wanted to start some writing. Jack said that he wasn't considering a creative project but would help us in whatever ways he could. We all wanted to learn more about the complexity of sibling grief. Aimee felt more accessible to each of us now, and we wanted to revisit our years with her in more depth. Perspective and wisdom were going to take time, perhaps years. But after our intense six weeks, we felt open to that process rather than intimidated by it.

During the summer Molly and I talked on the phone more often than we had since she left home for college. I felt more open and relaxed with her and slowly, my former feelings that I was imposing, interfering, interrupting faded. Molly was able to talk about her sister's illness and death, and in fact often initiated these topics. She was "in the middle of trying to figure out so much" and was "writing all the time." Molly and Jack communicated more frequently than they ever had before. I went to Brooklyn for an autumn visit around the time of her birthday, and while I was there, took more risks with asking questions and expressing my opinions. She talked about what was going on in her life in a new, less guarded manner.

Molly was quite supportive of my desire to write. She herself had started journaling when she was six-years old and had never stopped. She bought me notebooks and gave me a book about writing. She sent me writing prompts and guided me as I started on them. She advised me to express what I found emotionally important, even if I wasn't sure it was fitting together. She encouraged me to join a writing group. My daughter became my first writing mentor.

This interim time brought changes and adjustments for each of us. Jack started half time retirement at Purdue as he had planned. He became more relaxed and began expressing his feelings more openly. I started to think about retirement. I joined a writing group, went on a writers' retreat, and attended a workshop on memoir. Molly started some trauma resolution work and began accessing, acknowledging and exploring her anger and sadness. She said that our family work had allowed her to take this next step.

Over our 2010 Thanksgiving holiday in Pittsburgh, while eating brunch in a crowded café, we made the decision to do more therapy together over the upcoming holiday season. We all felt a need to check in with each other in a more extended way than our everyday lives in two different locations allowed. We all wanted more of that intense communication focused on helping Molly as a bereaved sibling and strengthening our family connections. Our time together would be more limited and our itinerary less ambitious, less structured. Molly's decision to do only occasional filming with her small, handheld camera eliminated the issue of equipment transport for her.

We had only a few weeks before her scheduled arrival in Indiana. The days flew by with all the extra time demands of the season. Our therapist was able to schedule us before and after holiday time with her family. In early December, Molly said she was experiencing intense feelings of sadness, regret, loneliness and anger that were confusing to feel all at once. The heartache I felt every Christmas season since

Aimee's death had already descended upon me, but it felt edgier and less contained this year. Jack was busy finishing up the semester with giving final exams and completing a research manuscript he wanted to submit before Molly's arrival. On December 20, he turned in his grades and headed down to the airport to pick her up while I finished putting up the last of the decorations and getting dinner together.

During that holiday season of 2010, we continued the therapeutic endeavor we had started earlier in the year. Much to my surprise, the primary emotion that I felt, even before our scheduled therapy sessions began, was anger, anger that Aimee had died and was no longer with us. It had worked its way into that time of deep darkness. Powerful feelings, inaccessible in the spring, were surfacing in me. Molly's clear challenge earlier in the year was that I *had* to be angry about Aimee's death. I hadn't been able to respond emotionally then, but anger expression over the holidays felt inevitable to me.

Molly herself seemed to be struggling with anger. It surfaced just before our first therapy session with her annoyance at Jack's focus on his computer problems rather than paying attention to emotions she was expressing about the demands of holiday preparations. My anger was biding its time a bit longer, finding little expression in our pre-Christmas therapy sessions. Was I trying to hold myself together before the holiday? Was it difficult to express anger in front of another professional? Did the content of the sessions themselves not trigger my anger? Questions I never answered for myself. However, during our several days' break from therapy, my anger finally manifested—at home.

During Christmas Eve dinner, in response to several comments Molly made, I pointed out a negative pattern that I observed in some of her relationships, certainly not my usual sort of holiday chit chat. I could see the annoyed reaction on her face and did a softened reframe of what I had said. Molly told me that I often made comments that were indirect but meant disapprovingly; they left her feeling criticized and guilty. I asked her what times she was talking about. She gave me vague feedback.

Heart Work

"Do you just want to see me happy all the time? Is that the only time you feel like you can communicate with me?"

"No, no, I know that you can't be happy all the time. That would be a totally unfair expectation on my part," I replied, knowing that some part of me would love to see Molly happy all the time, and, yes, that would make it easier to communicate.

I went on to ask her how she wanted to remember Aimee this Christmas, saying that she usually doesn't express much about this topic and that I found her impassive facial expression difficult to read and interpret.

"I don't care what we do tonight. Whatever we do is fine. I'll think more deeply into rituals for Christmas Day."

My sense was that Molly's response resonated with Jack, judging from his attentive facial expression and visual focus on her. A little later Molly told me that I was difficult to argue with, a complaint that I had heard before from Jack. I could feel myself shutting down, starting to cry, clueless about what to say. I started clearing off dishes; Molly helped and then left the kitchen.

"Are you ok, Mary Jane?" Jack asked.

"No, of course I'm not ok," I fired back.

I went down to our family room where I cried and wrote for nearly an hour. On my journal pages, I wondered how much of my anger was directly at Molly and how much of it was driven by an underlying sadness about Aimee's absence. I knew I needed to continue looking at my own behavior as well as my heartbreak over another Christmas without her. I also wanted to understand more about Molly's anger. I knew that I wasn't up to such explorations on this holiday eve. A glass of wine and tears weren't helping either. I felt confused about who I was as a mother, wanting the clear sense of identity that I felt when Aimee was alive, even though it was so intertwined with cancer and hope and attempting to live life under extraordinary conditions.

I went up to the living room where Jack, Molly and I ended up sitting close to our Christmas tree decorated with ornaments from across the decades—everything from the girls' early grade school creations to others I had needlepointed and ones we had received as gifts or bought to commemorate special occasions. The light from the fireplace created a glow on each of our faces as we talked about friends, relatives, places in New York, what we had done here in Indiana leading up to the holidays, which present we should open first. Without realizing it, I began tearfully talking about how much I missed Aimee. That was followed by Molly openly admitting how much she missed her sister, especially at the holidays. Jack said nothing, but for the first time on a Christmas Eve since Aimee's death, the three of us sat openly crying together over our loss and hugging each other in the reflection of the fireplace and the white lights on our tree. Our presence to each other felt so solid and so much more like an adult Christmas.

Jack and I woke up early on Christmas Day to fresh snow. I talked him out of shoveling in the dark, so early on Christmas morning. He agreed to read my journal instead, hoping to better understand what I had been feeling and thinking the night before.

"I have never witnessed you and Molly interacting in such an outwardly negative way. I'm worried about both of you."

We talked for a long time in the family room. Jack listened and tried to understand. Talking with him and remembering our time by the tree the night before helped calm me down.

After a reasonably tranquil Christmas day, dinner again became the arena for continued controversy. More accusations from Molly that I don't tell her what I'm really thinking and feeling, and that I convey judgments obliquely and then try to smooth them over.

"I probably don't have a good track record on speaking what I truly think to you, Molly," I admitted.

"I can believe that," she replied.

"Mom, why can't you simply say, 'That person has garish taste'?" she later asked when I was describing some decorations that seemed way over the top to me.

"That's just not who I am, Molly," I responded.

"But it's really basically what you mean, but you can't say it."

As we were finishing our meal, Molly said that she feared making statements that would not be taken seriously or simply get glossed over. I asked her if that had happened yet.

"Yes, Mom, it just happened in our therapy session a couple of days ago. I was talking about how when I was a kid, there wasn't time to just take a day off to stop and respond to my sadness."

In the session I had replied to Molly's statement by saying that I would have been happy to do that if I had known that she was really sad on a particular day—but that there wasn't much that she expressed emotionally. That statement seemed to really annoy her.

"So I am supposed to feel more guilt because I couldn't express myself as a kid!?" was her response. She went on to say that she was rewarded for being self-contained and not encouraged to be emotionally expressive.

Later Molly went out to a coffee shop, telling Jack that she needed a break from our quibbling. My daughter going out to a coffee shop by herself on Christmas night was beyond my tolerance level. My heart ached. I wondered if this round of therapy would make things worse. Perhaps all our seeming progress in the spring had been a sham.

On the other hand, I wondered if anger had worked its way into this emotionally charged time of the year because we were finally ready to experience and examine it, as awkward and unnerving as that felt. Was it anger toward each other for how we behaved or purely anger that Aimee wasn't here—or some confusing combination of both? My bet was on the third option.

Later I brooded by the fireplace and tree, neither seeming as magical as they had the night before. Perhaps clinging to old Christmas rituals was a way of keeping my anger under control as well as feeling a connection to Aimee. I was still puzzled about how to combine the holidays and grief. I had never wanted anger as the defining feature of either. Over the years, I had experienced sadness, longing, anguish, depression, resentment, emptiness and confusion. In the midst of all these painful feelings, I hadn't considered *not* being angry a problem. I thought it was a positive. I thought of it as bypassing the bitterness that so many people go through with a loss. And yet if the intensity of anger is in direct proportion to the loss, mine had to be enormous. How little I understood of myself. How uncomfortable old ways of being were starting to feel.

Gathering in the Heartland

Early in the next therapy session, one for mother and daughter, unanticipated anger swelled up in me when Molly repeated the statement that she felt rewarded for being self-contained rather than encouraged to be emotionally expressive. She said it felt taboo to talk in any detail about Aimee's disease and death. She was supposed to keep her chin up.

In contrast to her perceptions, I had thought of her as an emotionally expressive child and believed that we *had* encouraged self-expression in our home. She used the word "stoic" to describe Jack and me. I felt like we were anything but stoic, a descriptor I had never applied to myself. I felt like Molly didn't know or understand me at all. I instantly experienced the exact constriction in my chest and heaviness in my body that I had felt many times during Molly's high school years when I felt irrelevant and dispensable to her. I was transported back to the anger I had denied or ended up directing at Jack during that time.

Later that day as we began driving down I-65 to do some shopping in Indianapolis, raw feelings still festering in me, I began to scream and sob, spitting out an emphatic litany of complaints and resentments, past and present. I continued this behavior for most of the hour-long trip. Molly became the calm person, the listener and reasonable commenter.

Later that night she told me that she was grateful to me for expressing my feelings and that much of it needed to be said. I was thankful that I had finally spoken and that my irrational fear of Molly abandoning me had receded enough to allow this self-expression. It had not been pretty, nor did my psychotherapist ego approve of its form. However, it was genuine, honest and in the moment, even though, as I learned later, some of it was based on inaccurate information.

Yes, I had been angry at Molly, and she at me. We had been making judgments about each other for years. As therapy progressed, we discovered that sadness was beneath anger for both of us, sadness that Aimee hadn't been alive during those difficult years of adolescence. We both believed they would have gone better if she had been. In a larger sense, however, it was simply that Aimee wasn't here in all the ordinary and extraordinary ways that she had been, during the years we had been privileged to share with her. Later both of us admitted that this extended encounter, both in our therapy session and during our car trip, had created a stronger connection between the two of us. We had both been honest in our emotional expression even if not fully correct in our perceptions. We had moved into unacknowledged and frightening parts of ourselves, finally ready for expression in this time of upheaval and reconfiguration. Abandonment was not an option for either of us.

Life calmed down for us in the early days of the New Year. There was humor, concern and warmth. Therapy sessions became the container for our anger, anger we had come to view as a natural human response to our enormous loss. Molly and I were finally starting to acknowledge, express, and accept uncomfortable emotions as part of ourselves. As we moved forward with these efforts, Jack, who *had* been able to express anger, became the calmest family member. Our therapy sessions shifted to expressing our anguish over Aimee's death, sharing the dreams we each had had about her over the years, and recounting tender, amusing memories from both before and after leukemia.

We all warmly hugged at the airport. Molly had so much ahead of her in the next few weeks: starting a new job in New York, attending the Berlinale Talent Campus for promising young filmmakers, and waiting for the Academy Awards nominations to see if *GasLand*—she was a producer—had been nominated in the documentary category.

As difficult and painful as our grief work together had been, it felt like a true gift we had freely given to each other. It wasn't contained in a neatly wrapped and tied-up gift box, but something more like a recycled gift bag stuffed with wild strings of multicolored cellophane grass, flying in various directions, some of it trailing behind or spilled on the floor. It beckoned for rearrangement, sorting, clean up. I sensed that this effort would involve time, years of time. The disarray would be sitting there for a long while.

Chapter Three ~ *Wandering in the Wilderness*

> *A pilgrim is "one not at home," but I would contend that the pilgrim heart is where one becomes at home with being not at home; that is, the pilgrim heart is at home in the strangeness of the wilderness.*
>
> *In wilderness there is pain, and in pain there is compassion. In wilderness there is also beauty and the ability to see it large.*
>
> Sarah York, *Pilgrim Heart*

As our pilgrimage continued, the structure that had been so necessary for our therapy together shifted into an amorphous time of exploration on our own. Each of us was in an individualized but overlapping wilderness without a roadmap, involved in a process that was more instinctual than linear. What I describe here are my own personal wanderings in the wilderness which at times overlapped with those of Jack and Molly.

During this time, I felt led here and there. My intuition guided me to everything from a meaningful Rumi poem to a retreat on Exploring your Shadow. I started a collage in the crafts room that slowly expanded with visual representations of this phase of my life. I went to Centering Prayer, retreats, workshops, groups. I began expressing my emotions into a hand-held digital recorder when I walked. I rang our Tibetan bell every morning in gratitude for another day. I created a little altar in my office with rocks, shells, pictures, and a small bottle of oil from a St. Jude shrine. I drew, painted, colored, wrote down my dreams, read Jung and about Jung. I prayed a lot in multiple forms from Buddhist chants to Hail Mary's. Books arrived from interlibrary loan. Others were checked out from the library, some purchased locally or online—grief, siblings, sibling grief, the shadow, pilgrimage, death. I read, underlined, copied down quotes, often reread. I shared book titles with Molly who shared her titles with me.

I made time lines and outlines and lists. Notebooks and journals filled up one after another, and then lined up next to each other on the top bookshelf in my office. I also wrote on my computer. My folders and files became more and more complicated and required frequent reorganization, constant back-up. I poured over scrapbooks, my girls' art work, and medical records. I leaned on Jack, the most responsible, trustworthy man I know, and let him support me in all the ways he said he would. I talked to Molly, and Aimee. I drove over two hours each way once a month to see a Jungian analyst. I talked with my spiritual director monthly. I was equally drawn to the mystery of Catholic ritual, the social activism of the Unitarian church, and the possibility of dismissing all "isms" from my life. I walked under the early morning sky to my Tai Ji group listening to the grief playlist on my iPod. Tears streamed down the sides of my face in restorative yoga poses. I beseeched our beloved dead for their help, particularly when I walked past a neighborhood tree that looked like an angel with arms outstretched to heaven.

I became more contemplative and silent. I went online less frequently, deleted more emails, and turned off my phone for long stretches of the day. Both as a psychologist and a friend to myself, I wasn't worried. I knew that a major release of emotion and deep reorganization was going on inside me. I was determined to learn more about who I was and what my experience with loss had been. I had entered the Wilderness.

Ironically, I discovered unexplored resources right before my eyes, enough to occupy me for several years.

Interviews on cell phones

June 2, 2011

I sat in our favorite chair this morning, trying to figure out the next steps in our journey. Instead I found myself reflecting upon the chair itself.

We had very little furniture in the early years of our marriage. We moved a lot—Pittsburgh, Japan, California, Thailand—surviving with other peoples' furniture and a few basics of our own. When we moved to West Lafayette, with a tenure track job for Jack, we bought some furniture. Our first piece was dubbed 'The Chair.' It quickly became a sought-after spot in our home and has never abdicated this role. Its solid oak frame is angled slightly backward and padded with upholstered cushions. Sitting in the chair with feet propped up on its ottoman guaranteed instant comfort.

Initially we read newsmagazines and professional articles there. A year later, I sat pregnant with Aimee in the chair, feeling her movements and anticipating her birth. Later she and I sang lullabies, read books, recited nursery rhymes, laughed and chatted in the embrace of the chair.

Aimee held her new baby sister there. Later the girls sat in the chair together—laughing, singing, reading to each other or silently to themselves. They opened birthday presents in this place of honor. Our 1990 Christmas card was a photo of Aimee and Molly in the chair, both wearing caps in that year of relapse.

Now Jack sits there every morning after breakfast, drinking coffee and reading. When I want to think or read, I find myself there. The chair has survived both birth and death, all the while opening its comfort and witness to our lives.

Our therapeutic work together created an unease and curiosity in me that grew more intense during the months afterward. As I sat in the chair pondering how to direct these feelings constructively, my only insight was that talk and time would be involved. As more months passed by, I developed a stronger sense that unknown and unacknowledged parts of myself had been rattled by our grief work. By late spring, after more sitting and thinking, I formulated a plan for weekly phone calls with my daughter, focused on the post-therapy questions that were crowding the back pages and margins of my journal.

Initially Molly was resistant to the idea, claiming that speaking in person would be more effective. The impracticality of that approach shifted her reluctance over time, but not before we considered some of my questions face to face in her Brooklyn apartment, camera in attendance. We planned this session for my upcoming visit in June 2011 to attend a psychology conference in Manhattan. We decided to talk and film on Saturday afternoon when the conference was over.

As we were eating lunch before our session, we unexpectedly found ourselves discussing the hospital cafeteria episode from almost a year earlier. Initially I was talking about the morning workshop, trying to explain the complexities of a therapist and client attempting to communicate when both of them are in extreme states of psychological discomfort—the possible risks and merits of attempting to talk under those conditions, whether it's advisable to take that chance. Molly seemed intrigued by this discussion. I asked her if she thought there had been any times like this for us during our work together when we were both in extreme psychological discomfort and deciding whether or not to communicate. She immediately said yes, and began to talk about our lunch stop at the hospital cafeteria during our visit to the med center.

I myself hadn't thought of that episode in the context of what I was discussing. Molly explained that I had a certain look on my face when we walked into the cafeteria and then were selecting lunch items. It was the same look she had seen on my face during Aimee's illness and even more frequently after her death. She felt absolute terror that day as she had felt many times before when my face looked that way. To her it represented my simply not being there, not available for communication, lost in the world of my emotions. For her, it triggered the panicked feeling of being a child whose mother was not accessible. She said that anger came out of that sense of terror. There had been long phases of this terror/anger for her after Aimee died, she said, triggered by this facial expression of mine. She said those times were emotionally overwhelming and often numbing for her.

I was astounded, rattled and heartbroken to hear this.

I didn't know exactly what my face looked like at such times, but I did have a sense of what I felt like inside—confused, lost, abandoned, lonely, helpless—which must have translated into a facial expression that my daughter knew well. More importantly, I had no knowledge or recognition of its traumatic effect on my daughter.

Molly said that she had tried to process the hospital lunch episode with me in a therapy session soon after it happened. I told her that I couldn't remember her efforts and must not have comprehended what she was talking about. The mutual understanding we experienced had been long in coming. The realizations were profound. There was so much to know about each other, how we had affected each other, how little we may have known about ourselves, messages we had never meant to communicate and didn't know we had.

This discussion primed us for our afternoon filming session.

I focused on questions related to adolescence. Molly said that, as a teenager, she was depressed, alienated from her peers, lonely and angry, all in contrast to her notable academic success and a long history of having friends. She felt that she wasn't allowed to have these feelings in terms of family expectations. I had observed these shifts in her with great concern and discomfort, particularly during her junior and senior years, and began frantic efforts to intervene, few of which met with a positive response. I tried to talk with her, and when that did not work, I attempted a dialogue in writing. She went to therapy in her junior year. It didn't last long.

Molly said that she felt threatened by a mother who was a psychologist, especially as an only child and teenager. She said I was very indirect, but she still felt intimidated by my psychological lines of questioning. She suspected that I had an idea or theory about her and in reaction became very protective of herself. She described a chronic feeling during high school that she had done something wrong within the culture of our family.

We filmed for a difficult and emotional two hours. Molly spoke haltingly at times, often in sentence fragments. I was frequently tearful and searching for words from the numbness inside me. We both paused and reflected frequently. Molly said she felt sad for a couple of days afterwards. I felt sad too, and wondered why I had even asked Molly to do this. But she said she was glad that we had done it. I was too, despite how hard it had been. We agreed to talk more.

By autumn of 2011, we had decided upon and started a series of weekend phone conversations centered on my questions for her—clarifications, expansions, curiosities. We already knew that these talks would be painful sometimes and decided to put some parameters and boundaries in place. We agreed to talk for about an hour on weekends at a mutually agreeable time. We ended up having these discussions about every two weeks for a total of eight in all. Molly faithfully made the arrangements for when we would talk. We never just forgot. Our mutual commitment was a great source of comfort to me. I was the instigator here. I raised topics and questions, searching for information about our relationship and myself, information that I doubt Molly would have shared, had I not asked, had we not persisted and endured.

Basically I was interviewing Molly, returning to a format we had used in our original filmed work together. I sat in our beloved chair, my journal opened on my lap with its long list of numbered questions and blank pages for notes. My favorite gel pen was in my right hand and my cell phone was to the left on speaker phone. I never got through more than a few queries in our allotted hour. The topics were wide ranging. Do you think we could have done this therapeutic work any earlier? If Aimee hadn't died, how do you think you'd be different today? Did you see me as depressed after Aimee's death, and, if so, how did it manifest? What is the line for you between my sharing observations and my being critical? What did you see as common characteristics between you and Aimee? Tell me again about the magical thinking you did as Aimee became increasingly ill.

I sat in the chair afterwards, adding missing words to my notes and allowing our exchange of the day to sink in. I sat longer integrating new information that usually spawned even more questions to explore. Molly told me that she was emotionally exhausted after each session; I was too. It was very challenging work for both of us.

I was slowly learning to listen more objectively, to acknowledge but not fully buy into my emotional responses, and to accept what I heard as, at minimum, something to look into. I wanted to understand both myself and my daughter better. Molly revealed a lot about herself in these phone calls; her honesty and forthrightness were inspirational. I was talking to an articulate, reflective adult woman. My questions seemed to be tapping into pools of feelings and memories that were already in her awareness.

Molly said there were times while Aimee was ill when I seemed distant to her, like I was dealing with or thinking about something else. My immediate emotional reaction was defensive, feeling like I had worked very hard at meeting Molly's needs, being present to her, keeping her included in but not overwhelmed by her sister's treatment.

Wandering in the Wilderness

Almost as quickly, my mind was flooded with an inventory of issues and decisions related to Aimee's illness and managing our lives that, yes, did preoccupy me over the weeks and years. There were the touchy questions that recurred over time. Whether Aimee's immune system was strong enough for her to be in a crowd for a special event. If a friend's mild cold should keep her from going to a much anticipated get-together. The anguish I felt when the answer kept Aimee away from her friends.

There were broader life and death issues. Whether the current round of chemotherapy was really working. When and how we could best make the trip to Minnesota to investigate a bone marrow transplant. The question of whether a bone marrow transplant really offered us any better chance for survival than chemo.

Then there were the day-to-day issues. Figuring out who could get Molly to her dance lesson after school since we wouldn't be back from Aimee's appointment in time to take her, and Jack had to teach at that time of day. As much as I tried to compartmentalize my work and home lives, there were times when I was very concerned about a patient of mine or when an emergency phone call would awaken me in the middle of the night.

Yes, the times of paying attention to Molly probably coexisted with times of distraction and preoccupation. I was left wondering what this would be like for a young girl. I slowly began to accept that even though I had tried my best to be there for her when she as a child, she wouldn't necessarily have seen it that way.

Molly said that after Aimee's death she sensed that I was frightened of her growing up and perhaps terrified of her becoming older than her sister. We had touched on this topic in our initial therapy. In retrospect, I knew that I had had a difficult time with Molly growing up, particularly after eighth grade. She was such an endearing child and also my most palpable link to Aimee and to their relationship. It was difficult to let that child go, particularly while I was grieving the loss of another child, I who truly loved all those childhood years with my daughters. I didn't recall feeling terror when Molly became older than Aimee but rather an acute awareness of that approaching day, hour, minute. I remembered a sense of moving into entirely new territory.

Molly claimed that I have facial expressions and tones of voice that, in and of themselves, convey judgmental information to her. She said she picked up on them and ended up feeling anxious, suspicious and/or judged. I imagined that many daughters and sons could make similar observations about their mothers, but the context in which we were living added layers of complexity that many do not experience.

My daughter asserted that if anything, I'm overly polite and try to minimize discord. She saw conflict as part of being alive and at times very therapeutic, particularly when it results in examining inaccurate assumptions and starting to think and behave differently. She wondered aloud if all three of us avoided conflict when it came to family issues.

She believed that there were times when I used words but didn't express what I truly thought to her. I had been hearing various iterations of this statement throughout our work, particularly at Christmas. I decided that beneath these statements was a basic plea for more honest and direct communication from me. I wondered how ready each of us was for that, but also knew we had already moved in that direction.

Molly said that she saw Aimee's illness as really hard on Jack and me. At times she perceived me as sad and angry. She wished that we had all done this therapy with Aimee. All four of us had been in therapy of different kinds and lengths in the course of Aimee's illness or after her death—but never together as a family. A number of reasons for this churned around in my thoughts, including the fact that no one had ever recommended family therapy for us.

Rationalizations and explanations swelled up inside me across these interviews and topics, with a simultaneous gratitude that these issues had been spoken. There was a lot for me to take in here. Yes, I don't always fully express myself, and, yes, I know when I'm doing it. No, I don't like conflict. Old patterns for me, ones that seemed to serve me well even as a child. Molly was of little help in clarifying how my face looked or how my voice sounded in various upsetting experiences. This information felt irrelevant in light of the tentative openness that was developing between my daughter and me, a continuation and expansion of what we had started in therapy.

I had framed these interviews as an opportunity to learn more about myself, but I discovered a great deal about Molly across these two months. I became acutely aware of how sensitive she had been to all that went on around her, both when Aimee was alive and after she died. My view of her as a very well-adjusted child who did exceptionally well in such difficult circumstances clouded a fuller vision of her as the astute observer and masterful impression manager that she was. She said that she could remember routine events for our family like getting sandwiches at the deli near the hospital when Aimee would be drugged and non-communicative after treatment. Molly said she wouldn't ask questions and would try to act as if nothing was wrong. She learned to sense the mood of the family and the various phases of those moods. She was very affected by them and often couldn't quite connect the dots about what was going on. She said that she tried to bring about change during uncomfortable times, didn't realize that she couldn't always accomplish that, and felt guilty if she didn't. I had missed all of this.

I wondered how many of my behaviors, verbal and nonverbal, were my own efforts to prevent life from spinning out of control, part of my adaptation to Aimee's illness that over time became a part of me. Perhaps my face had expressed much more of my thoughts and feelings than I realized. I had even more to explore and accept about myself than I had anticipated.

As I learned more about who Molly was, I came to accept that she would not return to the carefree young person I thought she was before Aimee's death. Some irrational part of me had believed that she would. We moved into Adult Molly and Adult Mom communication, with the edgy challenge of incorporating more directness into it. I sensed that we'd be practicing for a long time.

I started to realize that the wilderness was neither far away nor particularly exotic. If I could experience it sitting in our oldest and most comfortable chair with just my journal, a pen and my mobile phone connected to my daughter's, there were probably other resources nearby, possibly within the confines of our home.

Diaries on a bottom bookshelf

July 16, 2011

>Over the years diaries accumulated on the bottom shelf of a tall bookcase in our bedroom, silent witnesses to my most intense years of childrearing. They came in a variety of prints—paisley, calico, geometrics, batik, sunflowers. Some had themes—cats and kittens, girls playing the piano, ballerinas. I chose new diaries each year either mindfully beforehand or on sale in January. Starting in late 1979, I wrote about one child for nearly four years, two children for over ten, and then one for another eight plus years. The diary collection was sealed in 2002 when Molly left for college.
>
>The diaries both intrigued and intimidated me. They were in no particular order, not even sorted out by daughter. I mostly ignored them, but smiled when I remembered they were there. Jack characterized the diaries as family treasures. He had backup copies made and stored them in a locked file cabinet at Purdue. For years I envisioned myself as an eighty something reading these volumes with calm, wisdom, and perspective.
>
>As Molly and I continued our telephone interviews, it struck me that these diaries were a primary resource to supplement and inform my memories. I pulled them off their shelf, sorted them into Aimee and Molly stacks, and arranged them in chronological order for each daughter. After reading a few random sentences, I felt the pull of this world of little girls, young women growing up in Indiana, my dear daughters.

Sorting and organizing the diaries were straightforward tasks. As I stacked and arranged them, I tried to remember when I decided to document our daughters' lives. I knew that our Lamaze teacher had strongly encouraged us to write up our birth experience. Jack and I did, soon after Aimee was born. I think I just kept going. Writing about her became an inherently satisfying part of life. When Molly was born, it felt natural to do the same for her. I hoped that each of our daughters would read her diaries some day for perspective on her life and the pure curiosity and fun of it. Maybe they would even do this diary exploration together.

Starting to read the words on these pages was quite another matter. I was afraid of all the emotions the diaries might stir up in me. I was afraid that the descriptions would be far from how I remembered those days. I was afraid that going through Aimee's illness and death again would pull me back into the raw numbness of early grief. At the same time, I was powerfully drawn to these volumes with a maternal curiosity and historical interest that over time won out. I wanted to broaden my perspective on those childrearing years after all our recent family work. I wanted context for Molly's arrival in the world and for Aimee's diagnosis and death. I wanted to see if the diaries held any clues for some of the differing perspectives that had come out in therapy. Most of all, I wanted to re-experience those precious years with my young daughters.

Two months later, I finally sat down in the chair on a bright September morning. I began. Aimee Mulvey Gandour, born on November 9, 1979 at 1:11 p.m., weight: 8 pounds, 6 ounces; length: 21 inches. On the second page were copies of her birth handprints and footprints. I instantly realized that I had a similar set from her death. My heart tightened. Deep breath. Keep going.

I did keep going and became totally engrossed. I was touched and amused, often laughed out loud or sighed in wonder. At a visceral level, I felt the deep love that so possesses and graces the lives of new parents. We adored our beautiful baby. We were fascinated by her facial expressions, smiles and even distress signals.

I was a grad student doing infant research at the time. As a neonate, Aimee stared for long stretches at the black and white faces and geometric designs I had constructed and hung up for her, inspired by some research articles I had studied. I carefully observed and documented her language development, motor progress, emotional expressiveness, and exploration of the environment. I appreciated the comfortable rhythm between her ability to amuse herself and her need to be held. She cried occasionally, mostly because she didn't want her bath to end or wanted to stay awake longer. Her smile felt social to me from a very early age. Rolling over, sitting up, crawling, walking—the expansiveness and euphoria of that first year of life.

I found a mother who cared deeply about her daughter and was thrilled to at last have a child. Jack was the loving presence and helpmate I thought he had been, equally enthralled with Aimee, and she with him. Jack and I truly worked as a team in caring for our daughter.

Around her first birthday, I wrote: "This first year has been miraculous. I can't imagine life without Aimee. She has brought such joy, awe and humor into our lives. We are so fortunate for her good health, temperament, and beauty. We love everything about her and know that the years will bring new complexities into our relationship, but she will always be a deeply loved human being. Raising her is a loving, creative project."

Reading the details of Aimee's early years comforted me. Memories washed over me while I was reading and afterwards. Joining a mother-toddler play group and meeting future best friends. Frequent embraces, kisses and family hugs. Picking green beans from our garden. Aimee's love of Sesame Street characters and our golden retriever. Books, puzzles, flashcards, crayons, and blocks. "Go pick up Daddy now," an imperative long before it was time to leave. Independence and determination—putting bath toys into the tub, climbing into her high chair, dressing and undressing, doing her alphabet puzzle over and over.

Days with these early diaries turned into weeks that opened up more sweet memories. Friends' birthday parties. Her love of nursery rhymes and Jack recording her breathless recitations from memory. Multiple "Let's talk about . . ." invitations from Aimee. Her swim and gym class at Purdue called DME (Development Movement Exercises). "Where does the sun live, Dad?" The exuberance of visits with grandparents, cousins, aunts, uncles. Bites out of a piece of bread followed by, "This is Virginia (or Illinois, Florida, etc.)." Her frequent laughter. She and her friend Erin starting the Purdue Lab Preschool together. Aimee wanting to help out with everything from washing the car to putting away groceries. The giant coloring book of *Twas the Night before Christmas* that she read and colored with her father for weeks before Christmas.

Wandering in the Wilderness

In 1983 shortly after we learned I was pregnant for the second time, my grandmother, Mary Donahue Reilly, died in Pennsylvania. We decided then that if our much anticipated, second child was a girl, we would name her some variant of Mary, perhaps the Gaelic, in honor of my grandmother and Jack's mother, also named Mary.

I wrote less about Aimee that year. I was determined to finish my prelims, a required step in my degree program, before our next baby was born, probably in October. Jack took Aimee to the first half of DME every Tuesday morning, and I did the second half. He picked her up from nursery school on Thursdays, and they spent the afternoon together while I did intakes at the psychology clinic. On the weekends, he took Aimee grocery shopping with him, and they often went on a bike ride. I knew with confidence that father and daughter would enjoy being together and that I could work with full concentration during that time.

At this point in reading the diaries, it struck me that none of what I had read so far was part of Molly's history. These volumes were about nearly four years with Aimee as an only child, our family as a different threesome.

As I read about Molly's birth, I remembered the connectedness and delight of those two disease-free years as a family of four with our two daughters. Despite the demands and adjustments of our expanded family, these years remain the most joyful of my life. I knew that Molly remembered little of her first two years. In my heart, however, I wanted her to remember them exactly as I did.

Molly's arrival and her interactions with us shifted our family energy in ways we all enjoyed. She entered the world of three firstborns and assumed her title of little sister. She officially elevated Aimee to the role of big sister and our family to a more substantive and complex unit. Molly was a gorgeous infant. Her seeming mission was to lighten us up. She started early with continuous smiles, enthusiastic greetings for each of us, and amusing facial expressions like the guilt inducing look she gave me when I settled her into her crib at night.

Once again I was thoroughly captivated with a daughter's infancy. I saw engagement as the hallmark feature of Molly's approach to her world. Sitting on her father's lap at the dinner table, she 'conversed' with Aimee, Jack and me by inserting babbling into the conversation whenever she could. She clearly saw herself as part of this family. Molly laughed out loud a lot, and her first word was "hi". When she sat in her infant seat, she carefully watched all the activity around her. As she studied the mobiles over her crib and my same black and white decorations on her walls, she kicked and vocalized, putting so much energy into her observations that she developed a bald spot on the back of her head.

Molly adapted easily to social situations and seemed to be stimulated by them. Sometimes when we were out, she would stare at people until they made eye contact and she could smile at them. She was very relaxed at her first swim lesson. Approaching people who came to our home seemed very natural for her. I wrote, "Oh, such a sociable, sweet, lovable little girl – so immediate and spontaneous. I'm awed, overwhelmed at times."

I was struck by how intertwined Aimee and Molly's lives were from the start, with Aimee staring into the eyes of her newborn sister on her lap soon after she was born. As an infant, Molly accompanied us on drop offs and pickups at Aimee's preschool. She herself was observed by students in the adjoining Infant Lab a few hours a week. Sitting in her stroller at her sister's DME class, she watched, smiled, and vocalized. Our longstanding mother-child play group, expanding with younger siblings, embraced Molly into its fold. She went to parties, picnics, farms, parks and museums as the younger sister. Once she learned to crawl, Molly consistently sought out the place of most activity in our home, usually where her big sister was playing a game, doing a puzzle or helping at the kitchen counter. When we introduced little pieces of table food to Molly, she would pound on her high chair tray for more if she really liked it, and Aimee would laugh. She was Molly's favorite audience.

As soon as she got up every morning, Aimee went into Molly's room to check on her. I would hear squeals, laughter and jabbering if she was already awake. Aimee spent time with her every afternoon, and Molly went along with anything her sister initiated. They would play fantasy games such as "going to a meeting" together. Aimee made noises and faces to make Molly laugh, demonstrated toys for her, paged through books with her. Sometimes Molly simply observed her sister for stretches of time, watching her do everything from coloring with markers to practicing 'run, run, run, leap' for her dance class. She touched Aimee's long dark hair, pulled at her barrettes, ran her fingers over their design, and then tried to remove them.

As I witnessed the deep roots of what had been lost, I felt both gratitude and pain. I developed a morning eagerness about what the diaries might reveal each day, a feeling similar to one many years ago when I anticipated the wonders of the day before the girls woke up. One afternoon as I was reading the diaries, I felt like both of them could burst into the living room full of chatter, and walk straight over to the chair where I was sitting. A few other days I felt like two little girls were in our house and that one or both of them might walk up, touch my hand and ask me a question. I expected to hear laughter or one of them calling out to the other. I felt joy and appreciation as I re-experienced those years; I felt reassured about the mother I had been. Sometimes I cried over the very idea of those sisters, my daughters.

1986: Initial Diagnosis

As I approached Aimee's initial diagnosis in the mid 80's, I resisted reading farther and set that diary aside for a week. Despite my avoidance, I still felt the heavy sadness of that time when our lives were altered in unimaginable ways.

When I resumed reading, I cried in a way I had never experienced in my life, not even after my daughter died. I had none of my normal sense that I was going to cry when suddenly oversized, heavy, globular tears would roll down my cheeks, splashing onto paper, my clothes, the chair I was sitting in. It felt as if they had traveled from far inside me, as if they had been patiently pooling, waiting, biding their time. These tears surprised me again and again as they reappeared in the days, months and years ahead. Was this water from the farthest depths of my grief well? Over time I came to believe it was. These tears were breaking open my heart in some new way.

Aimee was diagnosed with Acute Lymphoblastic Leukemia on a snowy day in late January of 1986, when she was six years old. There had been some intermittent joint pain the summer before and later in the fall. She had difficulty walking a couple of days in November and December, most notably around Christmas. There were multiple doctor visits and a tentative diagnosis of Juvenile Rheumatoid Arthritis. Further evaluation and an MRI at Riley Children's Hospital in Indianapolis took us to Hematology Clinic B and Arthur Provisor, MD on that winter diagnosis day. He became Aimee's hematologist, our guide and companion, for the rest of her life.

The disclosure of the diagnosis, the tears, the explanations, the encouragement, the consent forms for treatment, the social worker, the phone calls, the numbness are all a blur for me. I can't remember how Aimee was told about her disease, or how we explained it to Molly. I do remember a nurse's hand on my arm when I nearly fainted during the bone marrow aspiration that confirmed the diagnosis and placed Aimee on the Intermediate Risk treatment protocol.

Chemotherapy started immediately. With Aimee in a wheel chair, an IV trailing behind, we went straight from the outpatient hematology clinic to the inpatient pediatric unit upstairs. Later Jack and Molly went home to pack up necessities for Aimee and me. They returned the next day. I was in such a state of shock and so absorbed in the details of treatment that I wrote nothing about what was going on. Instead I filled in dates and numbers on Aimee's treatment protocol from the Children's Cancer Study Group, the roadmap for the next couple of years. I was so naïve about cancer treatment and its side effects that I didn't even realize that Aimee's hair would fall out until a nurse told me. Jack did have a history with cancer that went back to his sophomore year in college, before I knew him, when his beloved father was diagnosed with lympho-sarcoma and died 18 months later. A painful topic Jack mostly avoided. Now, a father himself, his emotions reawakened by his daughter's diagnosis. Cancer again.

Aimee's first hospital stay lasted for ten days. Even this early in treatment, the highlight of her day was time with the child life specialist who set up art projects for children on the unit.

Wandering in the Wilderness

Back home, I wrote in the diaries again. Reading those pages reminded me about how actively resistant to treatment Aimee became after we left the hospital.

"Why do I have to take this medicine? No one else I know has to take it. . . . I don't need to take this medicine anymore. I feel fine."

"Molly, I'm sorry I made you late for Toddler Lab because I couldn't take my medicine."

She said, "I can't," words we had never heard Aimee say. Explanations and pleading from us and others, a reward system, and an extended appointment at Dr. Provisor's office all occurred within two days. Aimee was still resistant. In desperation, I wrote her a note about *The Little Engine that Could* and then kept myself busy folding clothes and putting away dishes. In the midst of this, I heard her young voice repeating "I think I can" maybe a hundred times. She managed to start taking her medicine.

I began to see my emotions shifting on the pages. I often cried in the bathroom with the door locked. I burst into tears the second I got into the car for a trip to the pharmacy or grocery store. My agony was private, not in front of the girls if I could help it. Jack was worried about me; he saw me as "grief stricken". I thought about our therapy work with Molly and wondered about the facial expressions and moods that she had described, how far back they went, how tuned into them two little girls might have been.

Aimee responded well to treatment and was in remission within fourteen days. Sustaining this remission would involve another two and a half years of treatment. Her prognosis was Good.

"When my hair falls out and I look funny, I don't want to see anybody except Mommy." I asked Aimee what about her dad and sister. "Yeah, Daddy and Molly but nobody else."

"Don't touch me today. Just don't touch me." Or "I don't want you to kiss me," were orders that Aimee sometimes issued as chemotherapy progressed. It was not unusual to later hear, "I need a hug. Please come and give me a hug," which, of course, we did. Her medications contributed to the mood swings behind these confusing and contradictory messages. The confinement of her days and the dramatic changes in her appearance also affected her mood.

The ultimate barometer of Aimee's wellbeing was how well she and Molly played together. When Aimee was on massive doses of prednisone, her sister was the main target for unkindness, and Molly was just spunky enough to goad her on at times. Aimee would refuse to play, outwardly rejecting her sister, who reacted with tear-filled eyes and a downturned, quivering mouth. When Aimee was feeling better, she was full of gentleness and mothering for Molly who basked in her sister's attention and interaction.

About a month after Aimee's diagnosis, the girls finally played together several times over a weekend. Their interaction increased over time, and we began to hear laughter. It was so heartwarming to see the two of them playing with our dog, reading a book together on the floor, or chattering in imaginary play with Strawberry Shortcake and Blueberry Muffin.

During these months of intensive treatment for Aimee and unpredictable interactions between the sisters, Molly developed a relationship with an imaginary friend named Sally who would call her on the phone occasionally, or sometimes Molly would ask to call Sally. Jack pulled the cord out of the telephone and let Molly talk on it without having to hear a dial tone. Molly said that Sally was three years old and little, worked in Dad's department, and was her favorite babysitter. She had long chattering conversations with her and then might not mention her for days.

As predicted, Aimee's long dark hair thinned out dramatically, and she developed the swollen body and chipmunk cheeks characteristic of childhood leukemia patients. Late one afternoon her best friend Erin came over. Aimee told her that her hair was really falling out and then grabbed a clump, gave it a gentle pull, and out it came. Then another clump. Erin joined in. I stayed in the hallway as they laughed and giggled in Aimee's room, pulling out hair and piling it up on her bed. Before too long, there was little hair left on her head. In tears, I disappeared into another room, deeply heartened by the high-spirited way these two young women dealt with a moment we had all been dreading. At the same time, I was emotionally overwhelmed by this new challenge for Aimee. She wore a knit cap the rest of the day. As I was settling her into bed that night, she asked how long it would take for her hair to grow back. Our eyes exchanged a look of heavy sadness before we hugged each other good night.

By April, Aimee was well enough to return to school. As she was leaving one morning, I looked at her, smiled, and said, "It feels so good to see you go off to school each morning so happy." She got a puzzled look on her face, smiled a little, and then asked, "Oh, you mean because of all those days when I didn't go to school?"

I nodded yes.

She pulled on her Cabbage Patch backpack and with a full grin, off she went.

Around that same time, I was saying prayers with Aimee one evening and said, "Please, God, help our family to love each other and to make us strong." She immediately and emphatically stated, "We DO love each other, and we ARE strong."

I had forgotten about a second phase of Aimee's treatment protocol called Delayed Intensification following this brief break when she was very much herself. The diary jolted me back to that nightmarish return to chemotherapy, this time with worse side effects including even more dramatic mood swings and physical changes like a drop foot in her gait, a throat clearing tic, along with more hair loss and weight gain. "Mom, you feel different when you're fat—really different."

Aimee was very tuned into her body and reported detailed observations like: "Mom, there's a war going on again with my red blood cells. I can feel it in my legs." "My body feels like it's making new cells. My legs feel like they are fighting inside, and it hurts in my sides. I feel kind of tired."

As I continued to read, I felt the deep sadness of watching my young daughter suffer the side effects of poisonous medicines and struggle with her confusing emotions.

"Aimee, do you have feelings inside?" I asked one evening.

"Yes, some very bad feelings, but I'm not going to tell anyone what they are, no one."

Heart Work

Interestingly two days later when I asked her, "How are those bad feelings doing?" she started to tell me about them including: "Why do I have to have this disease anyway? No one else I know has it!" "It isn't fair; it just isn't fair." "You don't know the funny feeling I get inside when I see Dr. Provisor at the clinic on Fridays." "Sometimes I just wish I had something like a virus or a cold or something that would just go away in two or three days." "I don't look like a girl. I don't look like a boy either. I don't look like either thing." "Mom, I just wish everything would be the way it used to be."

She continued for some time. I listened, commenting sometimes. We both shed some tears. The next morning she said, "I told you a thousand things last night." I hugged her in gratitude.

When Aimee was going through this delayed intensification phase of treatment, Sally returned, this time with a presence in our home rather than at the other end of a telephone line. Molly would sometimes push her on our swing outside, and we would occasionally have to make room for her on the sofa. We neither dismissed Sally nor asked for detailed explanations about her. Psychologically I viewed Molly's imaginary friend as a creative, adaptive coping mechanism for a young child whose older sister was unavailable for a time.

I was reminded of Molly's comfort seeking. She'd say, "Rock me, Mommy," and we'd sit in our rocking chair with my arms and her "roar blanket" which had lions on its binding wrapped around her. We slowly rocked back and forth. It became an evening ritual for us. I think we both felt comforted by our physical closeness to each other.

I was surprised at how much I had written in Molly's diary after her sister's diagnosis and how little of it had to do with Aimee's treatment. I did write about Sally and how the girls were getting along at various points, but my entries were primarily focused on Molly's enthusiasm for preschool, her very social role there, and all the songs and rhymes she brought home to perform for us. Like her sister, she was very independent with clear messages of "I want to do it myself!" whether it was getting dressed, brushing her teeth or serving herself at the table. During the worst times of treatment, I think Molly kept me in touch with pre-cancer Aimee. And she made me laugh.

I was also very heartened by her unconditional love of Aimee and seeming obliviousness to all of her sister's physical changes.

"How did I get leukemia?" A question out of the blue at bedtime toward the end of delayed intensification. Not the first time Aimee had asked it. She continued on with questions that flowed one from the other with beautiful logic. "Would I have died if we hadn't gotten treatment?" "Which is worse – polio or leukemia?" "Are you sure I won't die from leukemia now that I've gotten treatment?" We talked. I answered as honestly as I could. She left no stone unturned.

We fully believed that Aimee would recover; she herself never seemed to doubt that she would. When she came off therapy in July of 1988, her hematologist wrote to her pediatrician: "We are delighted with her progress and look for her to remain in a disease free state."

Little did we know that we had just been through the least complicated and most successful of our treatment protocols.

1990: First Relapse

As I continued to read the diaries, I began to see the big picture and how succinctly time was segmented across Aimee's eight-year, two-month (1986–1994) struggle with leukemia. There was no such big picture when our family was living through this time interval.

The 1990 diaries began in the middle of those eight years. By then, we had been through Aimee's initial diagnosis, treatment, and years of remission. It had been a time of trauma followed by optimism and putting cancer treatment behind us. At the beginning of 1990, Aimee was a ten-year-old fourth grader and Molly a six-year-old kindergartner, each halfway through the school year. I saw both of them as exuberant participants in their childhoods.

Before I could move forward to read about Aimee's first relapse, in retrospect the turning point of our leukemia journey, I circled back to savor the last months of 1989 again. That autumn had been a time of particular joy and excitement for our family. Jack's brother Rich, his wife Jill and their daughter Rochelle, the girls' cousin who was Aimee's age, had moved to Bloomington for a year while Aunt Jill did a post doc at Indiana University. We enjoyed shared birthdays, our local Feast of the Hunters' Moon, Halloween, Thanksgiving and a trip to Kentucky together. The creative-daughters trio inevitably entertained us with shows and games during our get-togethers.

In addition, Aimee and Molly were at the same school, appropriately named Happy Hollow Elementary, for the only year that their grade levels overlapped in the same place. Each morning, the yellow school bus pulled up in front of our house where our girls boarded with the other neighborhood kids. I saw Aimee and Molly off every day and greeted them in the afternoon, except on Thursday when I had later appointments at my office. Jack was home for them then. I have colorful, sun-drenched memories of those sweet, disease-free days.

Aimee blossomed in fourth grade with a strong sense of her competencies. "Mom, I feel like I'm older," she stated in a very positive way as we talked about the beginning of school. Her hair was dark, thick, and just beneath her shoulders. She was involved in Girl Scouts, swimming, continued with piano, and started cello. She had also learned to play a Thai instrument, the khim.

Molly loved all-day kindergarten and grew in her sense of identity and self-esteem. She was involved in dance, gymnastics and later swimming. When she fell from our swing-set bars and broke her wrist that fall, she handled the aftermath with calm and bravery. She took her cast in for Show & Tell the day after it was removed.

Both of the girls did very well academically, had lots of friends, and enjoyed all sorts of activities. The sisters had their disagreements here and there, territorial disputes or power struggles of various kinds, healthy conflicts to my way of thinking, all part of the sibling contract for human growth. Essentially they idolized each other.

My heart tightened as I reached for Aimee's 1990 diary again and approached the hard-hitting news of relapse on January 2, 1990. After routine labs and a completely normal physical exam for Aimee that morning in Indianapolis, the girls and I headed home to continue enjoying the holiday break, expecting to get lab results later in the day. We weren't concerned about them. I happened to call Dr. Provisor's office after we got home to follow up on his brief mention of some ice-skating venues that his family enjoyed. On our drive home, we decided that it would be fun to get some friends together and go ice skating later in the week before returning to school the following Monday.

The nurse I spoke to said that she knew Dr. Provisor wanted to talk to us. After some initial pleasantries, he informed me that he didn't like what he saw in Aimee's lab work, and that he believed that she had relapsed. He wanted to see all of us early the next morning.

The news was shocking and incomprehensible to me, to Jack, and most of all to Aimee. She literally assumed a fetal position and cried uncontrollably after Jack and I talked with her. Our attempts at hugging and holding her seemed futile as sources of comfort. Molly sat on the sofa motionless, holding her doll. Her face looked frozen as she watched her sister so distraught and inconsolable. I sat there experiencing the heaviness, the sunken heart and unspeakable fear that my body remembered from hearing the initial diagnosis. More than anything, I was overwhelmed by the inescapable suffering that lay ahead for Aimee, already initiated by this new revelation.

The next day we left for Riley before dawn and watched the sun rise as we headed southeast to Indianapolis, listening to the soundtrack of *An American Tail*. The girls were together in the back seat, well behaved, busy making friendship bracelets, occasionally chatting, singing or laughing.

Dr. Provisor talked with all four of us. He said that even though we were going to start chemotherapy immediately, *it was not likely to provide long-term survival*. We heard the words; they did not fully penetrate even though they were repeated later in the morning. Aimee had a bone marrow aspiration, a heart test, a chest x-ray, and a spinal tap before starting her initial infusion of chemotherapy in the office. Jack, Molly and I went to the lab for blood tests to see if we were potential donors for a related bone marrow transplant for Aimee. With great disappointment, we found out later that none of us were.

A few days into treatment, Aimee told me that before the holiday break she had sensed something inside her that felt strange, but that she didn't know how to describe it then or now. Her legs also felt tired in PE class one day and soon buckled underneath her. I asked her if she connected it with leukemia. "No. I never thought my leukemia could come back," she answered.

My parents arrived from Pittsburgh to be with us. Aimee was so pleased: "Having Grandma and Papap here gives me energy."

There were changes in routine for us and a level of meticulous attention to the details of treatment that were new to Molly's awareness. The girls filled coloring books about leukemia with crayon strokes. Jack and I read children's books about cancer to them and tried to give explanations, probably as much for ourselves as our daughters. In hindsight, I don't believe any of these tools overrode the bewilderment that each of the girls felt in her own way.

On the way back from our next outpatient visit for IV drugs, I commented to Aimee that relapse chemotherapy was harder than her original treatment protocol. She looked at me, nodded affirmatively, and shortly afterwards fell asleep.

The pages of both of the girls' diaries validated that life went on. When school resumed, Aimee performed her parts in *A Christmas Carol*, a class performance delayed by bad weather before the break. Midweek, she and Erin came home after school to rehearse their lip sync for a friend's birthday party. When I came home Thursday night, Aimee was in bed but awake. She smiled warmly at me and said she had studied for her two tests the next day and was packed for her friend's birthday sleepover the next night. She and I both wanted lots of hugs.

Molly's life went on as well. At this point, she no longer needed her imaginary friend Sally because she had ready access to real friends who frequently invited her over. She also enjoyed her two new friends who had recently moved in next door. She continued to go to her dance class and finished her winter season of swimming. She became a major fan of *The Little Mermaid*. I noted in her diary that, as hard as we tried, I didn't feel like she was getting enough attention during this time. The content of the pages, however, argued we were clearly doing our best.

The girls were kind and loving to each other during those difficult weeks of early January, but over time, treatment and side effects increasingly took Aimee away from her sister. Some days the girls would both be off mood-wise, precipitating tears from them and occasionally me. "Sometimes I'm just so sensitive, and I let everything you guys say get on my nerves," was Aimee's explanation. At other times she was very loving and caring toward her sister: styling her hair, helping to get her book order together, fixing them a snack. These times provided a sense of normalcy for us.

In less than three weeks, Aimee's hair was falling out. She seemed resigned and stored it in a recycled quart-sized yogurt container on her nightstand. One night after we said some prayers together, I asked her what she wanted to add. After a pause, she said, "Just help."

By the end of January 1990, Aimee was in remission. Trying to keep her there would consume the rest of her life against odds that we had been warned about just a few weeks earlier.

I found a lot written about the creativity and consistency of Molly's efforts to keep her sister and the family buoyed up. During the initial months of treatment, she made a new Get Well Soon sign for Aimee at least once a week and also wrote a note to the family basically saying: *Dear Mom, Dad & Aimee, I love you all very much. I hope you get well soon, Aimee. Love, Molly.* She drew pictures of our family. Early on Aimee had hair, but soon Molly drew her with a scarf, varying the color from drawing to drawing just as Aimee varied her scarf colors from day to day. Molly drew rainbow after rainbow, some with darkness behind them.

Early in the year, Aimee had two hospitalizations. Molly went to school and mostly stayed at home with Jack. The diaries described trips to visit her sister at the hospital with familiar games and toys in her backpack; the daily phone calls back and forth; trade-offs that Jack and I made to give me some time at home, him some time at the hospital, and both of us time to be with each of the girls. Molly was right at her sister's side during a very challenging treatment situation in mid-February after the initial administration of a new drug in her protocol. After we got home, Aimee had extreme chills and vomited eleven times. Molly literally stayed by her side the entire day. She and I had talks about how her sister must feel.

As Aimee came out of those very challenging early months of treatment, we were amazed at her vitality and drive. She wrote multiple

Heart Work

thank you notes and started to resume her usual activities. She was Ramona the Brave in her class Book Week play. With her sister or friends or by herself, she painted heart-shaped boxes, decorated t-shirts, and learned calligraphy, origami, embroidery, basket weaving, and beading. One day after some difficult chemo, Aimee was sorting beads in her room. When I suggested she lie down, she said, "No, this is helping me."

She had to stop chemotherapy sometimes, either because of low immunity or compromised liver functioning. As threatening as these times felt, they provided more quality time for the sisters and allowed Aimee fuller participation in fourth grade. Aimee and Erin were thrilled when their History Day project *Moving through Time with Clocks* made it to the state competition. She won the school Citizenship Award, played the cello in her first strings orchestra concert, participated in the fourth grade musical *Tall Tales and Heroes*, had two pieces in the school art show, and participated in her class rocket launch.

Molly's kindergarten teacher said that she hadn't noticed any behavioral changes in her since Aimee's relapse and that Molly talked very openly about what was going on. She described her as a very secure child who was much sought after by others. She was getting ready for her first dance recital, swimming, riding her bike, and losing teeth. Molly read voraciously and started writing little stories of her own. Friends came to our house; she went to theirs.

As I read about these months, I felt like I was right back in 1990, living the ups and downs of this relapse. *I held on to every detail* and marveled at how the four of us had made it through.

In early June after school was out, at Dr. Provisor's suggestion, our family drove to Minneapolis to consult with physicians at the University of Minnesota Medical Center about bone marrow transplant options for Aimee. Photographs of the girls striking humorous poses in a sculpture garden camouflaged the somber nature of our mission. Two days after returning home, Aimee, Jack and I had a long talk about the seriousness of her illness and our limited options. She was quiet and sad.

"What does small chance mean? "

"What could happen to my liver?"

"I feel scared when I think that I might die."

Aimee became particularly affectionate and expressive during this time, frequently telling us she loved us and wanting to be hugged for a long time at night. She always kissed Molly good night when she went to bed at her earlier time. Then Aimee went in to kiss Molly good night again, before she herself headed to bed, even though her little sister was usually asleep by then.

In early summer, Aimee resumed chemotherapy after her liver functioning improved. She managed to get to Camp Little Red Door, a week-long cancer camp in southern Indiana, joyfully accompanied by her cousin Rochelle. By July, side effects from chemo were so severe that she could not attend Camp Tecumseh, a residential camp about an hour from our home that she had attended the year before and loved.

At Aimee and Erin's suggestion, Molly went to the week-long Straight Arrow YMCA Day Camp for the first time that summer. The night before, she reported feeling both excited and a little bit scared. She said she would be her usual self—a little shy at first, answering "yes" to questions, but by the end of the week she'd be answering, "YES!" She came home with daily reports about climbing, creeking, canoeing; she sang camp songs for us. We went to the family picnic at the end of camp, just Molly and I, because Aimee was ill from some of her meds. Molly was very accepting, saying, "We can all go next year."

In late August of 1990, the girls stood by our front door for their annual first day of school pictures. Molly, in her denim jumper with a big red bow in her hair, was full of excitement about starting first grade at Happy Hollow Elementary. Aimee was about to enter Burtsfield Elementary where students from the two younger elementary schools combined for fifth and sixth grade. Dressed in a madras plaid outfit with a matching scarf tied around her head, Aimee went off to fifth grade with confidence, curiosity and smiles despite her concerns about near baldness and a puffy face and stomach.

A week later, Aimee began the Maintenance phase of chemotherapy, which simplified her treatment regimen. Blood tests were at a lab ten minutes from our house. Medications were taken by mouth at home. Chemotherapy infusions in Indianapolis were reduced to once a month. These changes felt luxurious to us. If all went well, maintenance would be over in two years.

Between this simplification of treatment and our decision not to pursue a bone marrow transplant at this point, we sometimes forgot that Aimee was seriously ill. As 1990 blended into 1991 and early 1992, she continued on maintenance chemotherapy with no hospitalizations at all. There were better and worse days related to treatment and side effects, but leukemia became more the backdrop of our lives than a center stage character. Warnings that this treatment would not work for the long term silently bided their time in the wings.

I found that I had written voluminously about both girls in their diaries during this time.

During our 2010 family therapy with Molly as an adult, she described these years as a "wild and expansive" time when her world became a much larger place. She thought that the same was true for Aimee. Everything from Spacelab to Burtsfield TV for Aimee and "One Hundred Day" to horses for Molly. Her memory was that they both became very socially involved. Even grocery shopping with dad on Thursdays was exciting.

"I remember it all. I loved being seven and eight."

When I read the diaries from her first and second grades and Aimee's fifth and sixth, I came to appreciate the accuracy of Molly's description. I was impressed with her observational skills and ability to place both feelings and events in time and context. When I told her this, she said, "Mom, I lived through it." So did I, but Molly's perceptions enriched my memories of those two school years. Both girls had thrived, even with leukemia as a backdrop.

Aimee was 10–12 years old, in the fifth and sixth grade.

In fifth grade, performing in *Along the Heritage Trail*. Walking in the woods at Fifth Grade Camp. Getting the job done as class secretary. Making new friends, particularly Liz. Starting to wear glasses and feeling fashionable in them. Winning lots of awards at the end of the school year. Opening her eyes to science via her teacher who taught so lovingly and creatively: "Everyone wants to have Aimee as a friend. I myself would like to take her home."

Wandering in the Wilderness

When I was first sorting through the diaries, I found a cookbook of cookie recipes handwritten by Aimee around this time. She and her friend Kuleni invented these recipes and sometimes tried baking them after school. Fortunately they both had moms who allowed experimentation in their kitchens, and families who were willing to sample their products. My personal favorites were Oatmeal/Cinnamon Specialties and Tart 'n Tangy Lemon Cookies.

In sixth grade, working on a crew for BTV (Burtsfield Television). Designing and conducting a science experiment for the sixth grade Science Fair. Writing minutes as the secretary of Student Council. Representing her class on the school newspaper, the *Bobcat Bulletin*. A true gift of a teacher who empowered Aimee to accept and appreciate her intellectual and leadership talents. A class train trip to Chicago with most of the day at the Art Institute.

Challenges presented themselves. Aimee anguished over an early sixth-grade assignment, to write an essay about herself. Should she discuss her leukemia diagnosis or not? She decided not to and defined herself in ways other than her disease. Chemo had arrested puberty for her, leaving Aimee an outsider for many normal concerns of girls her age and giving her a younger look. Nonetheless she initiated discussions about menstruation and birth control with me.

Molly was 6–8 years old, in the first and second grade.

In first grade, telling me she was writing "a term paper" about Molly Pitcher. Talking frequently about a teddy bear hamster named Leonardo in her classroom. Playing soccer. Taking a dance class. Joining Brownies. Starting piano lessons. Winning the class award for cooperation. Loving her teacher who "makes things fun." At our parent conference, she described Molly as bright, sensitive, patient, aware, hardworking and creative.

One day as we were driving back from a Brownie trip to Maple Syrup Day at a state park, Molly was intensely reading a book called *How to be Funny* which in and of itself amused me. She watched our ice storm damaged crabapple tree get cut down with tears in her eyes. She was heartbroken that she had never gotten to climb it. She loved saddle shoes and wore them across these years. Molly was annoyed when a classmate made fun of her "too healthy" lunch.

In second grade, writing and drawing about the weekend every Monday morning in class. Using medical supplies to explain spinal taps for Show & Tell. All year long saying that her teacher was great. Enjoying soccer practices and games with O'Neil's Kelly Kickers. Asking questions non-stop: "How would you get rid of a boy you didn't like?" "Why do people get divorced after they say 'I do'?" "Why would they use an alcoholic beverage for the blood of Christ?"

Horses became a major interest in second grade. We made a Black Beauty costume for the Book Week parade. She brought in *Black Stallion* for Stop, Drop and Read Day and dressed as a jockey for Halloween. Aimee checked out horse books for her sister, because her school library had more than Molly's. When on her bike, Molly pretended she was riding a horse. She had a horse-themed 8th birthday party which included Horse Bingo devised by the sisters.

Jack routinely took the girls grocery shopping every Thursday while I worked at my office. They had become wise shoppers who could locate products, check freshness labels, and compare prices. After putting the groceries away, they went out for the junk food of the week. Afterwards Jack read out loud to them, usually from classics like *Heidi, Little Women, Anne of Green Gables,* and *The Diary of Anne Frank.*

At the suggestion of Dr. Provisor, the girls went to Camp Little Red Door together that year. Aimee taught Molly how to pack for camp, and we knew she'd look after her little sister. Molly told me that she probably wouldn't miss me until about 3:30 the next day. After this first experience away at an overnight camp, Molly described a funny feeling that she got inside "when I felt like I was going to cry." I identified it as homesickness for her.

Molly vigilantly watched her sister's activities during this time. Carefully following the program for the Spring Strings Orchestra Concert, monitoring every piece, telling us what was coming up next. Studying Aimee's softball games like a sports analyst. Going to her first swim meet, mimicking everything Aimee and Erin did, and accepting their mentoring.

Wandering in the Wilderness

More memories and details of the girls came alive for me. Aimee learning that her cello teacher had cancer, too. "I feel even closer to her now." Aimee and Molly both having a respiratory infection at the same time in winter 1991, a first time experience of being sick together that each of them cherished. One night at bedtime, Molly telling me that she loved Aimee and that, unlike some other brothers and sisters she knew, "the two of us don't hate each other and call each other names." The girls enjoying miniature golf in Florida and then designing a 9-hole golf course for us in our basement the day we got home. Molly creating numerous clubs with particular characters, languages, and dances for each. Aimee, with her own history of creating clubs, going along with them. Four hundred boxes of Girl Scout cookies in our family room— grouped, labeled and waiting for delivery by Aimee and Molly.

Would Aimee have lived with this same level of intensity if she had never been diagnosed with leukemia? Is there an altered state in which ill children live their lives? How would a healthy younger sibling have any sense of this? Did Molly think that she was supposed to help her sister maintain this intensity as well as imitate it herself? Or were both of the girls just naturally talented, creative and energetic, simply being who they were, leukemia or not?

Clearly Molly had been correct. This time greatly expanded the girls' sense of themselves in their world. It also helped to sustain Jack and me. We remained vigilant about Aimee's health and continued to consider the tough issues surrounding her disease. Simultaneously we felt the joy of indulging in the positive of our girls' lives as they grew and evolved across this stretch of time. Leukemia was always there, but so also was their sense of adventure and curiosity about life.

1992: Second Relapse

In December of 2011, I started the diary sections about Aimee's second relapse. I questioned whether I should even be reading these diaries. I had a cold sore, felt exhausted for days, and then developed a respiratory infection that lasted for weeks. During this stretch, I set aside the diaries. I wasn't sure when or how I would ever get back to them.

Eight weeks later, Jack and I were in Hong Kong where he was a visiting professor for two months. I had packed the diary copies from mid-1992 until Aimee's death. In the process of unpacking, I stacked them by year and daughter in a hallway closet. I was able to pick them up a few days later. This time away had been necessary. The dramatic change of venue helped.

In the reentry process, I began to comprehend the complexity of diary reading and the true wilderness I had entered. The *me of now* observing the *me of then*, both of them in flux, but only one of them knowing how these events would play out. Here I was, stripped of my full mothering role and responsibilities, re-experiencing what had happened so many years ago. When I tried to explain what I was going through with the diaries to Molly, her frame was, "Yes, it seems like you are going through something deep and important, Mom." Over time I felt the potential of this diary wilderness to expand and transform me. Simultaneously I feared that I might never get out.

July 13, 1992 was the last visit on the two-and-a-half-year treatment protocol for Aimee's first relapse. The day before, she had returned from two exciting weeks at Camp Tecumseh. Driving to Indianapolis, we kidded about impending growth spurts for her body, the freedom of no more treatment, what to do with that extra time and energy. She was twelve, about to enter junior high; Molly was eight, headed for third grade. After a normal physical exam and then a bone marrow aspiration, we waited in the exam room while Dr. Provisor examined her marrow sample. When he returned he said, "I don't like what I see. It's about 90% lymphoblasts."

We both knew that that meant another relapse. I burst into tears. Aimee's face went blank, and then tears welled up. I called Jack at home—silence, tears. About halfway through our sad and intense ride home, Aimee said she wanted to stick with her original plans to drive out to the girls' All Star softball game with her friend's family. "There will be food at the ball field, Mom," she reminded me. Aimee chose to go on with life as planned. Dr. Provisor called to talk to Jack while we were on our way home. Molly once again happened to be at her one week of summer day camp. She didn't learn the news until dinner time, tears flowing down her cheeks as Jack and I talked with her. Our family was to meet with Aimee's doctor the next day.

Wandering in the Wilderness

As we headed out the door early the next afternoon, Aimee turned to me and said, "Mom, we've done the same thing twice, and it hasn't worked. I think we better try something else."

"It's a bad leukemia," Dr. Provisor said, meaning that the markers on Aimee's cancer cells once again indicated a very poor prognosis. Our best possibility at this point was an unrelated bone marrow transplant, perhaps in six months. Aimee was scheduled for surgery later in the week to put in a central line that would allow for more direct administration of medications. She would be hospitalized for three days every three weeks for sixteen treatments or until she was in remission and had an unrelated match. Other drugs would be taken by mouth, injected at home, or administered at his office and sometimes our local clinic.

Molly looked wide-eyed and attentive during this meeting.

"Why don't we go to Heisei tonight?" Aimee asked on the way home. Heisei was our family's favorite Japanese restaurant. We did. Why not try to enjoy ourselves a little in the midst of all that was going on! Molly made supportive comments to her sister that evening and hugged her. She also looked very sad as she wrote in her diary. The next afternoon Molly made chocolate pudding, and she, Aimee and I sat outside on our front steps enjoying it.

Aimee said she just couldn't tell her friends about this relapse and asked if I could talk with their mothers. "Yes," and I did so in a series of difficult, tearful telephone conversations staggered across the rest of the day. The girls finished their 4-H projects and turned them in the afternoon before surgery. Aimee was quietly sad at dinner before playing her cello at the Strings Orchestra Ice Cream Social that evening. She saw some of her friends and then took a long bath when she came home. After numerous questions about surgery, she went to bed asking me to wake her up five minutes before we had to leave in the morning.

Molly was exhausted that night. She was reading in bed when I went in to talk and kiss her good night. I gave her a Purdue cheerleader troll and asked her to be a cheerleader for Aimee. I also told her to remember how much I loved her when she looked at the grin on this troll's silly face. She smiled at me. I knew I was going to be gone a lot more than I had been in the past.

On the way down to the hospital very early the next morning, Aimee and I talked the entire time—one of the most spontaneous, flowing, longest non-stop conversations we had ever had. We talked about Ben & Jerry's, the ice cream social, summer strings, the pieces the orchestra played, her fondness for playing the cello, her softball coach and summer as a catcher, the All Star team, popular music that she liked, what she was anticipating in seventh grade. Then we listened to and talked about excerpts from Bill Clinton's acceptance speech the night before. Jack got Molly off to camp that morning and would pick her up in the afternoon for a hospital visit with Aimee and me.

I started to sob soon after Aimee went into surgery even though I was listening to calming music. Later she looked beautiful to me in the recovery room. Chemo started that afternoon, soon after she was transported to her hospital room. Aimee had a lot of pain from a spinal tap; she also had a dramatic reaction to one of her chemo drugs. When Jack and Molly arrived, she was crying and vomiting. We all tried to comfort Aimee; eventually she fell asleep. Later Molly and Jack left for the Family Night closing ceremonies at her camp where Molly had a major role in a skit. Jack later told me she was great, "the loudest one."

He and I started devising arrangements of increasing complexity to maintain as much contact and stability in our family as we could. After the camp closing, Molly had gone home with Jack. They drove down for a visit late the next afternoon. In the evening, Molly and I went home together while Jack stayed with Aimee. The next evening I dropped Molly off for a sleepover with one of her friends; they were both starting soccer camp the next day. I headed down to the hospital, spent time with Jack and Aimee, and then he returned home.

After Aimee's surgery and initial reaction to chemotherapy, she had a smooth course over the next days. Her spirits soared when she talked to friends, her sister and relatives on the phone. I often went out in the hallway during these conversations. When I glanced through the window to her room, I felt comforted by the lovely smile I saw on her face as she chatted and listened.

Wandering in the Wilderness

After returning from the hospital, Aimee had energy, focus and enthusiasm. She was receiving so many gifts that she made a gift box for Molly. She told me that she didn't want her sister to become jealous of her. The All Star team won their next game. Having Aimee in the bleachers brought them luck, they said. I took the girls to a walk-in studio for a portrait before chemo did its obvious damage. I was worried that this was the beginning of the end.

As I read about this segment of Aimee's treatment, its intensity and unpredictability felt very present to me.

In late July of 1992 the downward spiral began, precipitating a hospitalization that was especially challenging, a precursor of future difficult treatment situations. After a slow start one morning, Aimee felt very tired late in the afternoon and developed a temperature that went higher as the evening progressed. Dr. Provisor told us to go to the hospital. We arrived after midnight, and she was admitted with a high fever, in severe pain, and with terrible mouth sores. We finally settled into bed about 3 a.m. After Jack arrived the next day, I went home.

As her condition improved, there were numerous phone calls back and forth between Aimee and Molly to catch up on what they had been doing. Molly had gone to see *A League of their Own* with her friends after going out for pizza. Her sister wanted to know all about it. Molly told her that she had cried six different times during the movie. After writing lots of thank you notes, Aimee had baked brownies with the child life specialist who later had a group session with her and two other patients. Both girls seemed pleased to be sharing their activities.

Over the weekend, Molly came down for a sleepover with Aimee and me to learn more about what the hospital was like. We ate frozen yogurt and watched the Barcelona Summer Olympics with drip IV chemotherapy going much of the time. In the morning Aimee had an irregular heartbeat in reaction to a medication. Suddenly and rapidly, electrocardiogram equipment and professionals trained to use it took over the room. Aimee was startled and frightened as were Molly and I. The episode lasted ten minutes, and Aimee became groggy. She slept much of the rest of the morning.

Heart Work

"Mom, if my heart stops beating, can they save me?" Aimee asked later. I answered "Yes" for her as well as for Molly and myself. Fortunately an alternative to this drug was available, and that situation never recurred.

As the hospital stay continued, Aimee's hair, which had been inching toward her shoulders, began falling out. Her low blood counts and the drug side effects were affecting her mood. She was thin, pale, and tortured with mouth sores. Finally, in early August, ten days after her admission and a few weeks before she was scheduled to start junior high, we drove home and were greeted by smiling friends who again had brought nourishing food for our family, finally together at home.

Aimee was exhausted. Even a simple trip to the grocery store was a major event. She said she just wanted to watch videos that she didn't have to think about. Our family was happy to be together, but we were all down and despondent. The next day Aimee cried in response to my comment that she was spending a lot of time brushing her teeth. Later, after the tears, she said, "Mom, I want to tell you why I think I take so long. I think that because I have my leukemia, I just don't want anything else to be wrong with me. I think my teeth have always been important to me, and so I'm trying to do all I can to keep them nice." Overall it ended up being a better day after we talked. We were happy to be home, no matter what else might be going on.

About a week later Aimee spiked another fever, and Dr. Provisor wanted to see her in his office the next day. She looked me straight in the eyes and said, "Mom, I don't want to go back to the hospital." Fortunately she wasn't admitted but did have a blood transfusion. The next day she had a lot more energy. She practiced *From a Distance* on the piano and went to a lesson for the first time since her relapse. Later the girls and I were talking about how much energy Aimee had since her transfusion with some new blood. I blurted out something about how if a bone marrow transplant works out well, a cancer patient's body can function a lot better. There were many questions from Aimee, and honest answers from me. For example: What could go wrong? What about graft versus host disease? What if the person wasn't a perfect enough match?

Wandering in the Wilderness

Later after I had gotten Molly settled into bed, I realized that Aimee was in her room lying on her bed sobbing. When I sat down next to her and asked what was wrong, she said, "I'm scared." We talked for a long time about how we had no guarantees with any treatment, but they were options to be considered. I rubbed her back and hugged her. She seemed to calm down. Later I heard her in the bathroom repeating, "I don't want to die" as she was brushing her teeth. It was absolutely heartbreaking to hear, but positive that she was expressing her feelings. I had never heard this level of emotional expression from Aimee about her disease before. My sense was that she had realized she could die and started to think of every possible way she could live.

"If there was some way to get all my bad cells together, how much space would they take up, Mom?" Aimee asked me one evening around the start of school.

"I'm not sure, Aimee. I really don't know."

"Well, is it like an arm's worth of leukemia cells?"

"Well, I know that a donor's bone marrow fits into just a few syringes. But I'm afraid we don't know how to separate out the bad cells from the good ones yet."

"I know that, Mom, but I thought it would be nice if we could get all the bad cells into my arm and then just chop it off and be done with it. I'd go for that. I really would. I could live fine as a handicapped person. I know I could."

We had three full weeks out of the hospital which was good timing for Aimee's junior high preparations—registration, picture ID, locating her classrooms, setting up her locker, going to orientation with her friends, buying some clothes and lots of hats. Molly was figuring out which school supplies she needed and which backpack and lunchbox would work out best. She and her friends were eagerly awaiting the letters announcing their third grade teacher and class roster.

At the end of the first week of junior high, I picked Aimee up from school midafternoon on Friday to begin her first weekend of chemotherapy in the hospital. It ended on Monday morning after a 5 a.m. IV infusion. We left as quickly as possible, got home in time to see Jack and Molly, have breakfast together, and all get out to school or work. The details varied and complications inevitably came along, but this basic treatment routine played out at varying intervals for many months. I think there was a lot of loneliness all the way around in our family. Hospitalizations separated us, and highly toxic drugs affected Aimee's mood and communication. After several months of treatment, she was still not in a solid remission.

During our family discussions so many years later, Molly told us that third grade was when things started to fall apart for her. Aimee's treatment became more intense then and took us away from home more often. She began to feel a real change, shifts in our family and sadness in herself. "I was doing dance, sports, normal things that I was able to do, but Aimee couldn't. So, in my mind, it was not okay to enjoy them."

My reaction was one of bafflement. Was she robbed of her childhood that early? But, of course, third grade began soon after this second relapse. Nonetheless I had thought of that year as positive for Molly. She seemed to be thriving in the ways we measure children in our society, looking at talents, achievements, friendships. I was looking at externals and missing the deep sensitivity and fear in my younger daughter whose older sister was often unavailable.

In this revelation from Molly and from reading the diaries, I began to comprehend how deeply her young life was impacted at this time, how her innocence was eroding, and yet how positive she was in the midst of it all. I was beginning to see the possible long term effects on Molly of the unpredictable nature of her sister's disease and her ongoing role as family cheerleader. Behind her big toothy smile and the uproarious laughter with her friends was a pain I hadn't been able to recognize and absorb at that time.

I pulled myself back to the diaries by focusing on one of the most exciting events of seventh grade for Aimee, her friend Marisa's Bat Mitzvah, which became entangled with the possibility of a bone marrow transplant. Aimee had addressed all the invitations for Marisa in calligraphy and planned to help her out more in the months ahead. In mid-February of 1993, we were notified that an unrelated bone marrow match had been found. Aimee was to be in Minnesota at the exact same time as the Bat Mitzvah. When our family talked about this at dinner,

Wandering in the Wilderness

Aimee left the table and burst into tears. She was heartbroken that she'd miss Marisa's celebration, but knew she had no choice in this situation. A few weeks later during a hospitalization, we learned that the donor had decided not to donate her or his marrow. We were all devastated. Aimee wrote a very angry letter to her potential donor, but never mailed it because of confidentiality. At this stage, no information could be shared about or between a possible donor and recipient.

Aimee decided to make a dress for the Bat Mitzvah since we couldn't find anything she liked in her size. She found a pattern, bought shiny purple fabric, and cut out the pieces the following weekend. She sewed whenever she had time, and took our old portable Singer sewing machine to the hospital to work on her dress there. She perched on the side of her hospital bed with the machine situated on her food tray pulled around in front of her. She finished hemming it on our way to Pittsburgh for my parents' 50th anniversary party and modeled it for her extended family. Closer to the event, she and Marisa worked on favors and name cards. Aimee found shoes and decorated a hat for herself. I would maintain that Marisa's Bat Mitzvah and a later one for her friend Liz were the social highlights of Aimee's fourteen years on this planet.

As I continued to read about these months of the 1992–1993 school year, I could see the shift in Aimee and Molly's relationship. Aimee wanted to spend time with her peers, quite normal for her age but an adjustment for Molly. She missed her sister when she was in the hospital, with friends, too ill to interact, or catching up on school work. Developmentally, the girls were in different places with a gap wider than those they had been able to accommodate in earlier years. Molly and I talked about this, but understanding did not take away the pain.

Nonetheless, the girls continued to be involved in each other's lives. Molly faithfully visited her sister in the hospital. Whenever possible, Aimee watched Molly's soccer games, dance recitals, and musical performances. Molly went to Aimee's strings concerts, art exhibits, and Spell Bowl competitions. The girls planned, prepared and served several elaborate dinners for their friends and our family. They played duets together at their annual piano recital in the spring. As always, they planned and enjoyed each other's birthday parties.

Early in the summer of 1993, Aimee thoroughly oriented Molly for her first stay at Camp Tecumseh and helped her pack. Then Aimee went off to Camp Little Red Door with her friend, Liz. After their return, she expressed concerns about her physical appearance: "I don't look like I'm thirteen." "People don't always treat me like I'm thirteen." "What if my body never develops?" "I saw some seventeen and eighteen year-old cancer patients at camp who looked younger than they are."

She asked if we could arrange three visits for later in the summer. She wanted to go to Florida to see Grandma Gandour; to Pennsylvania to be with Grandma and Papap Mulvey at their lake house; and for her cousin Rochelle to come to West Lafayette. All of these visits happened. Aimee was very physically affectionate to everyone—hugs, hand holding, arms around family members. She never labeled these visits as last wishes or this time as a last summer, but I found a clear statement that I had written in her diary: "Mom, we have to make the most of this time we all have together."

1993: Third Relapse, Investigational Drug

In October 1993 between Molly and Aimee's birthdays, the last they would celebrate together, the trajectory toward Aimee's death accelerated in ways we hadn't anticipated.

Grandma Gandour visited that month to "see the leaves," her code for hanging out with Aimee and Molly during autumn in Indiana. She enjoyed Molly's 10th birthday party with her friends and our family. In the evenings, she and the girls played games together in our family room. Excitement and laughter abounded. I specifically remembered the three of them playing *Scattergories Junior* and laughing hysterically, something about Grandma labeling herself a couch potato. We took her with us for Aimee's appointment with Dr. Provisor that week so that the two of them could meet. Molly stayed at school. We'd be back before the yellow school bus dropped her off.

After Aimee's exam and a bone marrow aspiration, her doctor dejectedly told us that she had had a major relapse. This horrible news was followed by intense emotions and a flurry of activity over the next week. Jack, Aimee and I returned to Dr. Provisor's office the following day. He presented three options: do nothing; try a high-risk, last

Wandering in the Wilderness

chemotherapy possibility; or do an investigational drug at the University of Minnesota. After exploring these choices together and having a conference call with the investigator, we went home to think and talk about all of this.

After explaining these options the best we were able, Molly asked, "Well, why *wouldn't* we do the treatment at Minnesota?" The third option made the most sense to everyone in our family, including Grandma. Aimee cried all evening. In the late night hours came her admission of fear, yes, fear of dying. I don't remember how we responded to this, what we did, what we said. Why didn't I write that down? I hope that our words were kind, loving and compassionate, accompanied by hugs and tears. I believe they were. I also think Molly was asleep by that time.

We waited for FDA and human subjects' approval. A football game, a movie, a trip to the airport for Grandma's departure. Aimee anointed with healing oil at a church gathering. Before we left, her friends delivered a sparkling sun-moon-stars shopping bag of small gifts to be opened over the course of Aimee's two-week hospitalization. They also left another bag of gifts for Molly to open during her week at home before she and Jack flew up to join us at the hospital.

Aimee and I sat in the rain on a small private jet about to take off for Minneapolis/St. Paul. This flight had been arranged by the Angels of Mercy who generously provided quick and free transportation for patients needing specialized treatment. It was too loud to talk. Aimee was sitting silently behind the pilots, eyes lowered, fingers against each other in a prayer position, listening to music on her Discman. I was in my own altered state seeking spiritual connectedness and guidance for the challenges ahead. A taxi driver met us when we landed and transported us to a streamlined hospital admission process. The staff was upbeat and caring. We settled in. Aimee's doctor was very intense and brilliant but also warm and funny. We liked him immediately, but mostly we hoped his research drug would work for her.

Aimee's hospital room looked out on the Mississippi River. I stayed there most of the time; Ronald McDonald House was my backup spot. For a couple of days, we were able to leave the hospital on two hour passes and took full advantage of that privilege. We bought beads, ate Thai, Italian and vegetarian food, and always stopped for the comfort of ice cream. As the days went by, Aimee unwrapped gifts from her friends according to their instructions. "Open right after you get to your hospital room." "Open after the second time you go to the bathroom." "Open after the third call you receive from a friend."

As treatment progressed, the pain began and traveled around her body—myalgias, a possible side effect of this medicine. Aimee unabashedly said, "Everything hurts! I need medicine." She vomited and couldn't eat. Later on we played Scrabble. Aimee watched cartoons and quiz shows, not her usual fare. Phone calls from friends and family helped to sustain us.

Several days into treatment, Aimee's doctor told us that the drugs were not having a major effect: "There would have been a more dramatic reduction in the percentage of lymphoblast cells in her peripheral blood by now if the treatment was working." He explained that some researchers hypothesize that cancer cells suicide when treatment is effective. When a cancer is refractory or unmanageable, something is wrong with that mechanism. After he left, Aimee talked about being very scared. Her level of faith in this treatment had been so high. Tears, sadness, disappointment for both of us, for all involved, here and at home.

In the midst of all our tears and anguish in the hours after this news, a volunteer appeared to take me shopping—something I had consented to days earlier and, under the circumstances, had completely forgotten about. Somehow in the moment, I decided that some time apart might be good for both of us. Very quickly I felt overwhelming unease being away from Aimee in what felt like a jungle of merchandise. We returned much sooner than planned.

When I entered her hospital room, Aimee was lying in bed clutching her purple bear and wearing a wooden cross around her neck, one she had made at an Easter activity. Her Turkish god's eye from Marisa was hanging on her IV pole. She was holding a small Indian sandalwood box I had given her. Inside it was a four-leaf clover on a piece of cotton. She told me that she had found it at Camp Little Red

Door two summers ago. She had surrounded herself with these meaningful symbols while I was gone. I didn't know she had brought them with her. She had also written in her diary.

> We were both emotionally overwhelmed.

I was emotionally overwhelmed reading about this in my diary.

> We lay in bed together and just cried for at least an hour. Aimee had gotten a roommate earlier, and we were behind a curtain. Then, at Aimee's initiation, talking interwove with crying. "Why is it that I have a disease that can kill me? Why not just one that could leave me with a handicap because I know I could deal with that?" She also said that she felt like she had so much to give: "Why should my life end?" She also described what she thought the meaning of her life was, "Maybe to show that you can live with adversity and hard times and still have a good and meaningful life." She talked about how some of her friends think life is a drag, but that she thinks it is wonderful and feels like she has had a wonderful life. She talked about her fears of dying and how she'd been thinking about science versus religion. I talked to her about my philosophy of death being somewhere between these two extremes. She seemed comforted. It was good to talk and cry. We were both relieved, I think. I couldn't remember Aimee ever being this open and expressive about death, her disease. She'd been thinking at a very deep level about all of this.
>
> The next day her doctor came in apologizing, saying he wished he were smarter and could help us more. He was more concrete and upbeat than the day before. "So, Mrs. Gandour, what are you thinking?" I told him that as a mom and speaking from my gut, I'd like to go home. He said that that was his assessment as well, but he needed to monitor Aimee's condition a couple more days. Later we could talk to determine our next step. We might learn that a second treatment could be helpful.
>
> Jack and Molly's flight arrived the next night through the high winds of late October in Minnesota. We were so glad to have them with us. The three of us slept at Ronald McDonald House and spent the next day at the hospital with Aimee amidst a flurry of Halloween activity on the unit. Later Molly and I ran a few errands while Jack and Aimee had

time together in her room. That night Aimee spiked a fever in the wee hours of the morning and was started on antibiotics.

Her doctor came in unexpectedly the next evening and began talking to Jack, Aimee and me about her treatment, his philosophy of medicine, and the ethics of continued treatment. His words were sobering but tender and caring. He did not paint an optimistic picture for Aimee's survival. I pulled him aside afterward and pointedly asked him how long he thought Aimee had to live. He hesitated and said, "I'd say about four months." Aimee lived five more months.

Molly had gone to the unit recreation room shortly before this physician came in. I wanted to go get her, but couldn't seem to act on this wish in the midst of the immediate gravity of this conversation. I have always regretted that Molly wasn't there with us.

Before we left West Lafayette, Aimee's friends had kiddingly told her not to come home unless she had gone to the Mall of America, then the largest mall in the world. Aimee wanted to go there. Jack's kind, generous and amusing cousin lived nearby and kindly volunteered to take us. Aimee's treatment team was willing to let her leave between her morning and afternoon antibiotics. We all did our best to have fun amidst the crowds and stimulation. Aimee was exhausted at the end.

We flew home the next day which was Halloween. Jack and Molly left on their earlier scheduled flight. Later standing at an airport ticket counter with Aimee in a wheelchair, I burst into tears over an irregularity with our tickets and the possibility that we wouldn't make it home that day. Aimee sweetly asked me if I needed a tissue. The scene must have been dramatic. Soon we were on the plane, and in first class.

At home, friends brought us comfort food and a basket of gourds, each painted as a caricature of one of Aimee's friends. We were grateful for this loving distraction from the sad news that we had brought home with us.

Aimee, Erin and Kuleni dressed up like witches and gave out candy at our front door for a while. Molly and her friend Ebba went out trick or treating in their Conehead masks.

After her friends left, Aimee seemed pleased to simply crawl into her own bed that night.

1993: November Respite

As I paged to the end of Aimee's 1993 diary, I found very little written in November, almost as if October had drained my energy and expressiveness. I wrote about her 14th birthday and Thanksgiving. When I dug out our calendar from that month, I saw Spell Bowl and piano for Aimee as well as scattered doctor's appointments and drug treatments locally.

She had a Mall of America sleepover for her birthday with games and puzzles that she and Molly had created. While we were at the Mega Mall, as the locals called it, we had picked up souvenirs and trinkets to use as prizes. Much of the party laughter focused on junior high stories. Aimee was weak, pale and thin but seemed to enjoy herself, mostly because she was at home with her friends and sister. She made it to school most of November.

We normally went to Pittsburgh for Thanksgiving, but just before this holiday in 1993, Aimee needed to be hospitalized on Wednesday until late Thanksgiving morning. We would be staying home. In response, my whole family decided to come out to Indiana. While Aimee and Jack were at the hospital, we all started cooking preparations together Wednesday night. Everyone was in charge of something, and there was lots of kidding and laughter.

Aimee and Jack arrived home early afternoon on Thanksgiving. She quickly started baking rolls shaped into rosettes. Aunt Laurie, my brother Ed's wife, wholeheartedly assisted Aimee with these creations. Somehow a scrumptious Thanksgiving dinner made its way to the table. It was a communal effort from an enthusiastic gathering of close family members who loved each other. We all sat around the dining room table, enjoying good conversation and lots of laughs. In the middle of dinner, my nephew Jason got up, went into the kitchen, and then came back to make a toast. His mother Laurie commented, "I think he's been to one too many Bar Mitzvahs!" I can't remember every word, but his toast was about "my cousin who is fighting hard and really trying." Everyone was touched.

After my family left, Aimee turned to us and said, "That was the best Thanksgiving!"

Final months 1993–1994: Hospital and Home

The next week was a very difficult one for Aimee—finishing a complicated math assignment, typing an English paper, performing in a strings recital, attending Molly's class musical and a friend's birthday. There were home antibiotics, mouth care and numerous pills. The following Saturday morning, she slept in, but that night Jack was driving her to the hospital with a temperature of 102 degrees. He said that Aimee was pretty shaken by the time she was admitted. He stayed overnight; we were in frequent contact. On Sunday afternoon Molly and I went down with some deli sandwiches and a few presents for my 49th birthday. Jack and Molly drove back home later. Aimee was having a very rough time with pain and was surly toward me. There were tears from both of us and then some resolution just as Liz's father arrived with five of Aimee's friends. The girls stayed for over an hour and a half—talking, laughing, hugging Aimee and each other before they left. Their energy helped to sideline Aimee's pain for a while.

The next morning she was calm and serene. After doing some schoolwork, she started making peppermint bead necklaces for her nurse and Molly. I went out briefly in the late afternoon on a bead and food mission only to return to Aimee writhing in pain. Morphine was not helping. Aimee's heart was beating irregularly, possibly doing what is called "a rub"—heart rubbing against the pericardial sac. After a flurry of phone calls between the staff and Dr. Provisor, she was scheduled for an x-ray and ultrasound. I called Jack to tell him I wasn't coming home for Molly's orchestra concert. We agreed that he'd come down afterwards. Molly went to our neighbors' house, but we later asked them to drive her down. We all needed to be together.

Dr. Provisor came to talk to us in the late evening. Aimee was crying and in terrible pain. Her pulse was nearly 150, tachycardia range. He called a cardiologist into the PICU. Before midnight this physician began trying to remove the fluid buildup around her heart using a needle. After an unsuccessful seventy-five minutes, he stopped. Molly arrived while this procedure was going on, and we tried to explain the situation and comfort her. She seemed puzzled and confused. The cardiologist said Aimee would be ok for the night. A cardiothoracic surgeon would talk to us in the morning. A mini PICU was set up in our hospital room with Aimee's nurse on one side of the bed and me on the other. She slept calmly.

In the morning Aimee wanted her beads and got busy with them right away. Just as she was expecting breakfast, a 'no food' order came because of possible surgery before we had even talked to a surgeon. Later he wanted a decision before we had even consulted with Aimee's doctor. Jack and I talked and debated. We thought out loud to our trusted nurses. We finally got to hear the familiar voices of Dr. Provisor and our very kind infectious disease doctor. We had questions about putting Aimee through a major procedure with no guarantees of what the outcome might be. When we realized that Aimee would die in a couple of days if we didn't act, plans moved ahead.

I know that Molly was around that day, that she slept later than usual after getting to bed so late. I remember her as an observer of her sister's suffering and all the decision making. I don't remember her speaking up.

Early the next morning, the three of us went down to surgery with Aimee. Wide doors opened, and she was pushed into a vast hallway with people moving very rapidly here and there. A head cover was put on her, and she disappeared. I wanted to crash through the doors and run alongside of her speaking soothing and gentle thoughts. Other patients were lined up on gurneys—like planes waiting to take off at a busy airport. The three of us sat together, hoping and praying, our eyes focused on the colorful holiday lights in the darkness outside.

The procedures, a pericardiectomy and lung biopsy, were over quickly. The surgeon and Dr. Provisor greeted us in scrubs. Fluid removed. Lung biopsy done. "It went well."

She had excellent care in the PICU, particularly from a nurse who was an ardent Purdue fan. Aimee made gentle headshakes in response to our questions. With time she had more facial expression and ability to move her body. She gestured for pencil and paper and began rapidly writing questions that we answered. She moved on to writing comments as well.

Aimee was off the ventilator and on oxygen late the next morning. Her voice was raspy but got stronger as the day went on. We all ate our favorite frozen yogurt together when she was allowed to have food. After Molly and Jack headed home, Aimee sat in a chair and talking to friends on the phone. The next day, a Saturday, we moved back to our regular room, 504, where we so often stayed when Aimee was admitted. By now it felt like *our* room.

The lung biopsy from surgery indicated that Aimee had pulmonary and pericardial Aspergillus (fungal pneumonia), much more difficult to treat than its bacterial counterpart.

Time went on. Room 504 filled up with Christmas decorations. Aimee's friends brought her a little tree, each of them pictured on one of the ornaments. A pair of red silk pajamas and a Christmas CD appeared from the generosity of her evening nurse. Measures of her physical wellbeing slowly improved. One afternoon Aimee accused me of thinking that she was a nuisance. I was getting on her nerves.

In my 1993 Aimee diary, I mentioned a letter she had written to the junior high during this hospital stay, saying that she would not be returning to school. A friend of mine sent us a copy in the mail in case we hadn't seen it. To this day, I am not exactly sure how it got to school and distributed. I had no idea that she had written this letter. Many years later I was able to see it as an indirect statement on Aimee's part that she was going to die (see Appendix C).

Hospice care had been arranged before we left the hospital on December 20 with Aimee on oxygen. My complete lack of experience with death and dying prompted me to ask her treatment team as we departed, "How will I know if she's dying?" Something about changes in respiratory patterns and the promise that hospice would help me with that. We were given a letter for the coroner in case she died at home so that there would not be an investigation. I was numb.

At home Aimee was surrounded by medical equipment—an IV pole, an oxygen tank, a portable toilet. The dressing on her incision needed to be changed daily. An antifungal medication was to be administered every other day by IV along with fluids for hydration; an injection was also to be given on those days. Nine other drugs were to be taken by mouth in various combinations at five different times spanning early morning until 11p.m. Over the next days, kind and skilled hospice nurses modeled and taught me the procedures I needed to learn for Aimee's care. She herself paid meticulous attention to every word and each demonstration. I never heard the word *death* uttered in the midst of all this teaching. We were locked into a strict schedule with little margin for error. I created checklists, schedules and reminders.

A freezing cold January followed. The pale blue walls of Aimee's bedroom coupled with the intense sunlight, sparkling snow, and clear blue sky outside often created an otherworldly feel in this space. My body felt leaden. Getting myself invigorated in the morning, usually my high energy time, was difficult. I had serious medical responsibilities and felt exceedingly sad. Initially Aimee slept about twelve hours a day and had little energy when she woke up. Our school district had a speaker phone system wired into her bedroom in case she wanted to listen in on a class. Aimee was lonely, and I intuited that she was tired of being with me so much.

As the weeks went on, she gradually went out more, increased her food intake, decreased her morphine, and became more alert. Her friends called, and she called them. Aimee watched movies, played games, read about Gilda Radner, beaded necklaces, baked cakes and cookies, wrote letters, and watched basketball games with the family, 'babysat' Molly if Jack and I needed to make an appearance at a reception or dinner. Aimee said she had too much time on her hands, and felt isolated and antsy. She wanted to start piano lessons again.

We continued to have weekly appointments in Indianapolis. On January 10, 1994, after a bone marrow aspiration, we learned that Aimee was in remission, which her doctor labeled "miraculous!" We were in a state of shock—puzzled and overjoyed. Two weeks later the surgeon said that her incision looked "wonderful." Her infectious disease doctor was "amazed." Her blood counts were good. She went to the junior high for lunch a couple of days later. The next week her doctor pronounced Aimee "a medical wonder."

Less than a month after hospice had begun, Aimee no longer qualified for this care.

By the end of January she wanted to try a half day at school, and her doctor gave permission if she felt up to it. On February 1, Aimee got herself ready, packed her lunch, and went off to school, her first time there in nearly two months. She came home energized. Erin asked Aimee to accompany her on the piano for a cello contest the next weekend. After half days for the rest of the week, she went out to lunch with her friends and in the evening went to *Schindler's List* with them and a friend's mother. She gladly accompanied Erin on Saturday.

Aimee wanted to go to school full days the next week. Jack and I were reluctant for her to take that leap, and the level of tension in our home over this issue was high. She told us that we didn't know her body and that staying home made her more depressed. When I picked her up early afternoon on Monday for her Indianapolis appointment, she was pleased that she had gotten to preside over the Student Council meeting—she was president, after all—and said that registration materials for high school had been distributed that morning.

We let her try a full day on Tuesday. It went well. After school she and Erin were at our house obsessing about high school classes. Later that week, Jack and I went to the parent meeting about registration with a sense of unreality. Aimee was being very efficient about getting homework done, relaxing a bit, and getting to bed around 10 p.m.

She made it through four full days at school that week and the next. Her friends and classmates were incredibly loyal and loving. The teachers, staff and administrators could not have been more caring or accommodating. Nonetheless, reconnecting with her junior high life was challenging while she was also feeling her *dis*connection from it. She realized that Valentine's Day at school was now just for couples. Classmates cared about music she hadn't caught up with yet. Friends played sports that she couldn't possibly do. Her peers were leading a very different life than she was. I think she felt the pain of that realization. One night when Aimee came home from a junior high event, she tearfully said, "I just wish I could be normal."

Despite these challenges, Aimee started the last week of February in a very positive mood and with her appearance improving. I picked her up for our Indy appointment, and two hours later we learned that she had relapsed. 80% lymphoblasts! Tears, sadness, "Why?"

"I'm confused about everything," Aimee cried out as we all sat down at home that evening. Tears and confusion were dominant for all of us. The next week involved a lot of decision making. The first decision was the more straightforward one. She turned down a Make-A-Wish Foundation trip to Disney World in part because we had already been there during a Florida visit to Grandma Gandour's years ago. She explained that she felt grateful to all the people who had worked hard to make this offer, but in her heart she simply wanted to stay at home, go to school, take the eighth grade assessment tests, and relax with us over spring break.

The next decision was heavy, life threatening, and rife with risk. Should we pursue the last possible chemo option, a highly toxic agent, or let Aimee's leukemia continue to take over her body? The possibility of overwhelming infection was high with both options. Jack and I were reluctant to do more chemo. After a long and complicated conversation with her doctor, Aimee stated her position very clearly and emphatically: "If I die, I want to know that I did absolutely everything that I could to try to stay alive."

Our spring break was bookended by chemotherapy in the hospital on both weekends. As soon as we arrived, Aimee set up her sewing machine and began assembling a colorful patchwork of printed fabric squares she had cut out at home—vegetables, sunflowers, sun and moon, cats, pizza, Thai batik, kitchen utensils, fish, and flowers— all expressive of her likes. On Sunday, Jack picked Molly up from a friend's birthday sleepover at a hotel in Indianapolis. She joined us for the afternoon and then stayed overnight with Aimee and me. Dr. Provisor kidded her about going from the Radisson to a hospital room. So far, so good.

When we got home, we wheeled the IV pole back into Aimee's room. Between these two long weekend chemo treatments, we had a busy medication schedule to maintain. Before settling in, we ran out to buy iron-on plastic to line the patchwork bag she was making for Erin. Aimee and Molly interacted a lot during those three days at home with no real schedule except for meds and blood work. They slept in and went from puzzles to reading to beading to cooking. One afternoon I took pictures of them sitting in front of our fireplace, rays of sunlight from a nearby window shining on them both in an otherworldly way. A day later, we returned to the hospital for another long weekend.

"Aimee is doing well," I wrote as we headed into what turned out to be Aimee's last week at home and school.

She was just too tired for Monday morning classes after treatment but went to school for lunch and afternoon classes. After her weekly appointment on Tuesday, she had to go get platelets. Aimee had a lot of energy on Wednesday which felt like a nice, normal school day. She played her cello in the pre-contest orchestra performance that evening. After school on Thursday, dressed in green for St. Patrick's Day, we went for a blood draw at our local clinic, did an IV drug infusion at home, and then went to our annual St. Paddy's Day celebration with the O'Callaghan-Diekman family. On Friday, Aimee went to school again; Jack took her to Indy for more platelets in the late afternoon. She played in the regional orchestra competition that evening and went to the celebratory pizza party afterwards. She wasn't home until after midnight.

Midmorning on Saturday, she, Erin and her mother met us at Molly's Purdue History Day. Afterwards we all went to lunch at the Memorial Union. Aimee was very tired when we got home and went upstairs to take a nap. She mentioned that she'd like to have lentils and rice, one of her favorite Lebanese dishes, for dinner that evening which we did. At 4:30 a.m. on Sunday, Aimee came into our room saying she wasn't feeling well. In the early afternoon we drove her to the hospital with a rapidly escalating fever. Aimee died less than a week later.

March 1994: Aimee's Death

As I turned the blank pages remaining in my 1994 journal for Aimee, I found nothing written about her passing. Once again the extremely intense not documented. The story of her death, however, was and is an indelible part of my oral history of the time and of our family.

All four of us were at the hospital and had spent a relaxing Thursday evening together, munching on snacks and watching the

Purdue-Kansas game with a win that got our team into the Elite Eight. Afterwards we reminisced about the girls picking raspberries outside for their breakfast when they were little, the creek that ran through the yard at our old house, and the clubs Molly had invented and her older sister agreed to join. Aimee talked to her friends on the phone. Liz was at a musical at Purdue; Aimee left her a message.

The days before had been very rough—high fever, diarrhea, a nosebleed, pain, lack of appetite, shortness of breath. Mid-week came a diagnosis of Acute Respiratory Distress Syndrome. I had seen the x-ray of her right lung seeming to fold in on itself but had great difficulty associating it with my daughter's body. By Thursday evening, Aimee was on oxygen, but somehow our evening time together felt soothing. Our whole family slept in Room 504 that night.

"I can't breathe, Mom," were the words that woke me up. We watched a flurry of medical activity envelop our daughter/sister and swoop her down the hallway in her bed toward the PICU. We exited the room, running as close to Aimee as we possibly could. And then she quickly disappeared into intensive care.

Only later were we allowed to go in and be with her—sedated, hooked up to monitors, seemingly peaceful, silent except for her breathing, never to speak words to us again. We surrounded her, holding her hands, touching her arms and shoulders, kissing her, hugging her, silently begging for the grace or magic that could bring her fully back to us. Crying, all of us crying, and feeling like Aimee was crying right along with us. Saying her name repeatedly, imagining her saying ours. Especially Molly crying and repeating Aimee's name. My arm around Molly. Somewhere in the midst of this, a chaplain and the Last Rites.

We *could* speak and *did* all that day and the next—about how much we loved her, how much fun our life with Aimee had been, how kind, loving, creative and intelligent she was, how much she meant to us as part of our family, what a good sister she was, how much we had learned about life from her, how courageous she was, that we would always remember her, how much she meant to us, what a good daughter she was, how fortunate we all had been to be in a family with her, how much we would miss her, and over and over, interspersed everywhere, how much we loved her. That we would always remember and love her.

Two nurses who were very close to us stopped by the PICU whenever they were able. Another nurse who had frequently taken care of Aimee during our extended December hospitalization walked in unexpectedly Saturday afternoon. She never worked weekend shifts at the hospital. She had not called to see how Aimee was doing and did not know how close to death she was. This nurse had been outside cleaning up her wooded property, and something just told her to go to the hospital. She arrived in old muddy boots and dirty clothes. She came to our side.

Erin arrived. We let her be alone with her lifetime friend. From the hallway, we could tell that she was tearfully talking to Aimee in the animated voice of their usual interactions. And then we waited for her close friend Liz to arrive. We had told Aimee several times that she was coming, and finally she got there. More time with a tearful friend. When she stood up to leave, all of Aimee's monitors changed. As Liz and her parents hugged us goodbye in the hallway, a nurse told Molly, Jack and me that we'd better get in there quickly.

Aimee died an hour later.

A female rabbi said a gorgeous prayer that completely matched our feelings and the situation. I later asked her for a copy. She said that her words came from simply looking at all of us. She was not exactly sure what she had said, nor were we. The nurse who intuited that she needed to be at the hospital helped us each to hold Aimee in a pieta position, something I came to understand only then – the heaviness, the deadness, the anguish. We washed Aimee's body together. She assisted Molly with making several prints of her sister's hands and feet. We talked to Aimee as if she were there. Her sacred body that had been through so much and had supported her survival for so many years was there with us. Her spirit was also hanging around for sure. We could feel it. We lingered with and talked to Aimee for as long as we possibly could until the mortuary staff could wait no longer to remove her body. One of the nurses told me that the saddest occasion in all of her work was watching a family depart after the death of a child.

Wandering in the Wilderness
1994–2002: After Aimee's Death

When I started to read about Molly in the years after Aimee's death, I was struck by how much there was to read, how many years had gone by for her, living in this home and community without her sister. That time felt shorter to me while we were living it, but the quantitative measures of calendar days, words, and pages argued otherwise. A timeless fog rested upon the otherwise crisp boundaries of school semesters, dance sessions, sports seasons, and family events. It struck me that the time span was almost exactly equivalent to Aimee's eight years with cancer.

During my first read through, I felt buried under the sheer volume of information and the raw emotions stirred up inside me. These later diaries had a metrical rhythm and concrete style to them. They contained fewer quotations, less humor. I was unable to formulate a larger picture as I read along probably because the woman writing these words was unable to formulate a larger picture of life. I no longer had Aimee's diaries as a counterpoint or supplement to what I was reading about Molly. I intuitively knew that I would remain in this Wilderness for an extended time with these diaries about my younger daughter.

Molly returned to school a few days after her sister's funeral, starting with a half day. She had Aimee's same fourth grade teacher, a loving and comforting presence for all of us. Soon ballet, French club, and horseback riding worked their way back into her life. She played *Dona Nobis Pacem* (*Grant us Peace*) at the annual piano recital, dedicated to Aimee that spring. Teacher conference comments about Molly's academic abilities, personality, patience, and care of other students were heartening. Friends invited Molly over. Aimee's friends kept in touch.

All three of us admitted to feeling very downhearted and sad.

In addition to Aimee's grand funeral in West Lafayette, a simple memorial was held for her at the hospital chapel a few weeks later, primarily for medical professionals who had known and cared for her over the years. Dr. Provisor gave the eulogy and talked about the beautiful relationship between Aimee and Molly describing them as *alter egos* for each other. As I double-checked the meaning of that term,

I was struck by how they *had* been alter egos in every sense: another side of oneself, a second self; an intimate friend or a constant companion; a very close, trusted friend who seems almost a part of you.

Given the girls' closeness and shared experiences over the years, the loss of her sister was everywhere for Molly—in our house, her school, so many places in this town, even in our car and yard. In the occasions of life and our times with extended family. Of great significance, Molly had lost her confidante, audience, role model, teacher, ambassador, wise woman, and co-creator. With these losses, she had lost parts of herself: the collaborator, admirer, student, conspirator, empathizer, entertainer, and co-creator. These descriptors are simple first passes at the enormity and complexity of what Molly lost when her sister died. During this diary reading in the wilderness, I could see Molly's losses more clearly, right there on the pages.

In her 1994 diary, there were images of grief across life situations. Molly's sad expression after school, a usual check-in time with her sister and me over a snack. The restlessness on Friday night, a time when she and Aimee were often together, particularly before junior high and her second relapse. Subdued excitement after her spring ballet performance without her sister's hug, congratulations, and flowers. The mixture of joy and pain when we attended Kuleni's Confirmation. The awkward loneliness of the last day of school without Aimee and an end-of-the-year photo of the two of them.

I recalled hugging, commenting, acknowledging and smiling sympathetically during times of discomfort, and then frantically trying to soften Molly's pain by doing something together like reading, cooking or going out somewhere. The diaries reassured me that during this time, I was wise enough to notice signs and attempt a caring maternal response. They also reminded me that I couldn't take Molly's pain away any better than I was able to take away my own.

I wondered what else I had been doing during that time. Trying to survive, I imagine. I remembered the cafeteria facial expression that had been so triggering to Molly. It had to have been around then. I wasn't able to read or write about grief or death for many months but knew that I had journaled frantically at the keyboard six to nine months after Aimee's death. I finally found a copy of those entries. The words felt commonplace to me when I wrote them so long ago, simple and honest reflections on my internal states. These unedited pages can be found in Appendix D.

During the summer after Aimee's death, I found days, weeks and months of activities for Molly, probably a peak time of busyness. As I read about all these goings-on, I felt overwhelmed. At the time, I was glad to see Molly experiencing so much, having so many friendships, and connecting to life despite her sister's death. Activity and achievement continued in the years ahead.

In therapy with us as an adult, Molly expressed her need as a child for more down time and a less scheduled life. The activities themselves didn't seem to be the issue; Molly appeared to love them all. I think she was expressing something about the larger matter of honoring sadness, loneliness, confusing emotions, and unanswerable questions by providing the time, space and inactivity to be together or alone in simple ways during times of emotional need.

I had allowed Aimee to stay home when she was overly tired, suffering from side effects, or trying to catch up. Often it was a mutual decision and sometimes one that I insisted upon. The emotional turmoil of Molly's grief was much less obvious to me than her sister's extreme physical symptoms. I was conscious of Molly's heartbreak and did my best to respond when I recognized it. At her young age, she wasn't able to verbalize all her feelings and probably felt very confused by them. She may also have sensed that we were simply trying to make it through the days and assumed that we were not up to the task of supporting her in all the ways she would have liked.

My 1994 diary entries about Molly stirred up more memories about her grief during this time. Her *Lonely but Learning* composition for a fifth grade assignment to describe a scary incident and what you learned from it. An essay on death that she sent to *American Girl* magazine. An emotional lunch she, Erin and I had in Indianapolis with the treasured nurse who had guided our family through beautiful rituals after Aimee's death. A visit to the fifth floor of the hospital for an emotional reconnection with her care providers. Our family attending

Heart Work

Year of the Family vespers at the local cathedral for families who had lost children in recent years.

As I continued to read about this time after Aimee's death, I felt and re-appreciated the sense of community around some marker events of that first year. For Aimee's 15th birthday in November 1994, we invited friends to bring bulbs to plant at the cemetery. Molly helped us to plant ours. When Aimee's one-year death date came around in March 1995, multiple blossoms from these bulbs comforted those of us gathered to bless her gravestone. That same day we planted another October Glory maple tree—"Aimee's Tree"—this one by the Creative Arts Center at Camp Tecumseh where she had learned many of the crafts that had helped to sustain her. Family and friends surrounded this tree and offered gifts of music and poetry, some of it read by Molly.

The summer before eighth grade, Molly decided to move into her sister's room. The sky blue walls changed to off white. We painted the sliding closet doors with Crayola black paint, turning them into a blackboard surface that friends could write on with chalk. Up went a colorful celestial wallpaper border. Molly painted some of its motifs on the blackboard corners and attached glow in the dark stars to the ceiling. Over time the space began to feel like hers. She moved in on the eve of Aimee's 18th birthday in November. A month earlier Molly had celebrated her 14th birthday as an eighth grader. Was there anything conscious about this timing? Not on my part. Molly had no memory of these seemingly calculated ages and dates when I asked her about them.

That school year (1997–1998) brought more loss and transitions for our family. It would have been Aimee's senior year in high school. Molly lost a beloved uncle and an iconic grandfather. My brother died in September. Uncle Tom bought the girls everything from flashy old purses to antique music boxes at Pittsburgh auctions. He loved making them laugh especially at the lake while we sat on the deck. My father died four months later in January. Papap, a tall, blue-eyed, white-haired Irishman, had started Tomanetti Food Products in the 1950's and became mayor of his town in the 1970's. He was a source of laughter, wisdom, attention, and mutual admiration in our family, particularly for his grandchildren.

Wandering in the Wilderness

My mother's dementia worsened. I went to Pittsburgh frequently to help with the sick, the dying, the dead, as well as the papers, possessions, and dwellings left behind. My brother Ed and I assumed our roles as family survivors, discovering that we solved problems well together. We made difficult decisions about our family members and eventually the small business our father had started and our brother had owned in the years before his unexpected death.

For Molly, her mother was again gone intermittently for days, sometimes unexpectedly in response to stressful situations. Jack and Molly were again by themselves sometimes. There were phone calls to stay in touch. I cried every time I left home, and then again every time I left Pittsburgh. Sometimes I drove; sometimes I flew. It made no difference in terms of the tears.

Molly told me that she missed me, but continued with all of her schoolwork and activities. Jack was the loving, reliable husband I could always depend upon. Friends rallied to help us out as they always had. Molly never complained and welcomed me warmly every time I returned. She and Jack came to Pittsburgh for visits and funerals

On February 22, 1998 in the darkness of the wee hours of the morning, Molly became older than Aimee who had died when she was a bit over fourteen years and four months old. Had Molly calculated that time as I had? During those spring months, the sense that Molly was older than Aimee was palpable but unspoken for all three of us.

In May of Molly's eighth grade year, Aimee's class held a National Marrow Donor Registry drive to honor and remember her as they were about to graduate. Her photo and story were on a large bulletin board in the junior/senior high school. Our local newspaper and TV channel encouraged participation. The organizers wisely asked Molly to organize a raffle to raise money for this event. She completely threw herself into this project and recruited her eighth grade classmates to help. With tremendous enthusiasm, they convinced community businesses to donate prizes, sold multiple raffle tickets, and provided entertaining commentary between drawings for prizes. During this all-morning event in the school gymnasium, hundreds of potential donors lined up to join the registry. Molly worked tirelessly on this project to honor her sister. She was exhausted but flying high after it was over: "I feel really good!"

As an adult, Molly told us she always anticipated what would happen at each grade level through her sister's reports and confidences. Aimee had mentored her younger sister in this regard through eighth grade, and in a larger sense had modeled life for Molly until then. I believe that Aimee was alive in some sense for Molly until the end of her eighth grade year.

Molly and a male classmate won the Citizenship Awards for the junior high that year. At the school awards evening, she received academic recognition in every subject and won a merit award for orchestra. She had a flower sketch done in pastels chosen for a local student art show. Four years after her sister's death, she was heading off for the challenging world of accelerated classes in senior high. She seemed ready for that transition.

The high school years, however, were disorienting for all of us. Behind our family smiles were parents who hadn't experienced adolescence with their older daughter, and a bereaved sister without the role model she had always had. The teenage years involve struggles for most parents and their daughters and sons, no matter what the circumstances. But for us, grief complicated adolescence; adolescence complicated grief. Both complicated parenting.

None of us was prepared for high school without Aimee.

Molly started as the MORP queen (prom spelled backwards). She sewed pink ribbons onto her new ballet toe shoes, designed her science experiment for biology class, and won the Aimee Gandour Memorial Award. She ended high school as a National Merit finalist and a valedictorian.

I saw Molly as intelligent, talented and beautiful. She was independent and had a wide range of interests, friends and activities. Sleepovers, dances, movies, boyfriends, hanging out with friends, and service projects were all part of life. She went on camp and youth group trips that took her hiking in the Rockies, white river rafting in North Carolina, and skiing in Michigan. As a Lafayette Ballet Company member, she performed multiple roles in *The Nutcracker*. She played her violin in the high school strings orchestra, except for junior year when she opted for Photography—"I'm not leaving this high school without taking an art class."

As time went by, an entire wall in Molly's room became a collage of *Rolling Stone* front covers, pictures of musical artists like Dylan and Bjork, photos of joyful moments with her friends and some with her sister. In the midst of it all was a piece of butcher paper decorated with bright spirals, butterflies and flowers. On it Molly had printed, "You're going to die. The real question is if you'll truly LIVE." The statement felt directed to herself and anyone else who read it.

Despite this challenge to truly live, grief gauze still separated me from my daughter at times, wrapped layer upon layer around me, to help cushion her from the full weight of my feelings. She herself had her own opaque grief gauze, tightly and carefully bound around her, sometimes concealing her struggles completely as she engaged in the developmental, academic and social challenges that come with high school. Jack's grief gauze had a scratchy texture, uncomfortable to the touch sometimes, but well shielded by outer layers of reliability and responsibility. Each of us was wrapped and trapped in a unique way, none of them particularly effective in the long run.

Unspoken for me was the question of what these years would have been like for Aimee, and what they would have been like for Molly, had Aimee still been alive. I think I sometimes felt like Molly was going to high school for both of them.

We had our power struggles, mostly in the second half of high school, debates about privileges, occasional confrontations. We weren't used to them. I wasn't able to see the humor or normalcy in those times or to simply step back in wisdom. I sometimes got myself trapped between Molly and Jack, creating further pain and polarization in our family.

This discomfort manifested in the diaries, rarely as a central theme but in ways more subtle and awkward. As I read, I was pulled back to Molly's statements during our 2011 filming session in Brooklyn about feeling alienated from her peers, depressed, angry and lonely in high school. The diaries documented that I sensed her pain and felt concern about it. I tried to talk with her while I rubbed her back late in the evening or when we were driving alone in the car. She occasionally opened up a little, but overall my efforts were unsuccessful.

Ironically, at work people paid for talk time with me.

When verbal communication wasn't working, both Jack and I tried writing to her. During our therapy, Molly disclosed that she often felt judged, trapped, or cut off in these letters. She perceived them as well intentioned efforts to communicate but ineffective at engaging her. She didn't think we heard her responses and so she stopped trying to present her point of view. I found some of those letters in my computer files. I felt like someone else had written them, not me.

As I pushed on through the high school diaries, I couldn't figure out what was coming from adolescence, from grief, or from some interaction of the two. Clear distinctions weren't apparent. And Molly was right about my attitude toward her in high school. I did want to see her happy.

I kept reading and was pulled deeper into my own pain and confusion about those years. Once again my longstanding view of Molly as a well-adjusted person who handled challenging situations well prevented me from seeing her deep struggles more accurately. She had lost parts of herself that she needed during those years of trying to find self. Even the superficial aspects of adolescence had to be challenging for her. After all that she had been through, her tolerance for normative drama over teenage catastrophes had to be quite low. How could a friend's breakup with her boyfriend or a team losing a game compare with the death of her sister? She also knew, all too well, that people you love deeply can suddenly leave you. Yet, eternal friendship was believable for most of her peers. I imagine that in the midst of her grief, Molly missed some aspects of adolescent growth.

But the situation was even more complicated. As an adult, Molly explained that in adolescence she had a chronic feeling that she had done something wrong. What? It was subtle, involved a high standard, "thought crimes", "emotional crimes", crimes of not wanting to act a certain way. Her perception was that she couldn't fulfill the family expectations for her, an ideal that she saw offering very little room for the upsetting emotions within her.

I couldn't remember articulating family expectations, but did words need to be involved? Was having confusing feelings and expressing them *not* to be valued in our family? Had we really conveyed that to her? I thought about our deep discomforts of grief, Jack's and mine, so unspoken and unexpressed to Molly who had been the antidote to dark emotions within our family for years. What Molly was feeling as a teenager had a depth and complexity to it that, from her point of view, would have made it exceedingly difficult to process with us, her parents—the supposed perpetrators of the expectations.

For weeks, I was distracted by thoughts, feelings and questions related to those later years of high school. I thought I had let all of that go. I became increasingly convinced that we could only have done this work with Molly as an adult. Wasn't this the slow and painful reparative toil that we were incapable of doing during high school? Wasn't our recent willingness to dwell in the uneasiness and awkwardness of expressing our feelings part of what brought healing to our family?

I finally pulled myself back. I wanted to finish the diaries. I returned to 2001.

My mother was edging toward death as Molly moved toward graduation. I continued visiting Pittsburgh to spend time with her and assist my brother and his wife with issues related to her care. At difficult crossroads, Molly listened, lovingly responded to me, and offered deep insights. I was with my mother when she died, once again breathing a last breath with someone I deeply loved. Ruth Reilly Mulvey died right in the middle of Molly's senior year. The unshakable and unconditional love of maternal grandparents became a memory.

Molly's last semester of high school wound down with lots of invitations to parties, the norm for how our community celebrated its graduating seniors. We had a great one at our home, which included people from across the entire spectrum of Molly's life from her piano teacher to relatives who traveled to West Lafayette and classmates she had known for years. She said that she felt some sense of connection to everyone in her class. Graduation was a real high for us.

Heart Work

As I read about the summer before Molly went to college, I remembered my distinct sense that another daughter was about to die. I cried privately every few days. Instead of discussing my feelings with Molly, I would be quietly angry if she wasn't home for a special meal I had prepared or feel annoyed when she wasn't making progress on assembling dorm room necessities.

Molly left home to begin college in September of 2002, all of us driving northeast in a van stuffed with selected possessions. What I remember most vividly from the parent orientation in Providence was a dean's bit of advice: "Expectations mean the death of serenity," a statement encouraging parents to allow their sons and daughters to follow their own paths during the intense years ahead and further suggesting that doing so had benefits for parental peace of mind.

The diaries I kept on Molly ended there, just as our emotional goodbye at her dorm closed a chapter in our parenting. The suggested parental work on our own serenity felt like a new opening to us.

Reading the diaries generated powerful feelings in me that resonated with the situations on their pages and felt familiar to me. The words stimulated fuller memories and fleshed out particular times with enhanced richness and specificity. The diaries brought gifts to me, like words my girls had spoken as children and the larger picture of what had happened over the course of Aimee and Molly's lives. In going over these volumes as much as I did, I incorporated those years more fully into who I am and saw our therapeutic work with greater clarity.

I had a difficult time letting go of the diary component of the Wilderness. I'm not sure I really wanted to. Before I attempted to leave, I had written hundreds of pages about each of my daughters and filed them away in folders with titles and an organizational scheme probably obvious only to me. I came to know each of them, all of us, in a more complex and human way through this reading and writing. I love the four of us even more.

These volumes, arranged in chronological order by daughter, are neatly lined up on their original bookshelf, waiting for that woman in her eighties to slowly and gratefully review them again, embracing and loving their insights and questions— perhaps finding some new ones.

Wandering in the Wilderness

Medical information in accordion files
My Hero

Dr. Provisor is my hero;
He helps me with Leukemia.
Although he hurts me all the time,
He helps me get better, so it's fine.

When I was in the hospital,
I would cry and I could squeal.
But all the time that he is there
I am getting better, so it's a deal.

When I go down to Riley each week,
There are machines that go zip and tweak.
And since I'm eating like a horse,
It seems that I am getting worse.

But all that medicine and stuff
All of a sudden will go puff,
And all because of Dr. Provisor
I'll be better, that's for sure.

Aimee Gandour
January, 1990
Two weeks after her first relapse

Toward the end of reading my diaries from Aimee and Molly's young lives, I wondered what other unexamined resources might also be right here at home. I had stored away a lot from Aimee's life and death—everything from selected clothes to all the cards and notes we received after her passing. Items with particular meaning for family and friends were given to them. Over time I carefully sorted, grouped and consolidated all that remained, placing most of it in clear plastic bins. These stuffed containers, along with some clothes on hangers and some bulging accordion files, eventually found their way to the closet in Molly's old bedroom which had become Jack's office.

Heart Work

The closet's sliding door was partially blocked by a heavy, butcher block table that had been in our kitchen when Aimee was alive. It was weighted down with computer accessories. Jack was able to slant the table out far enough for me to slide open the door and reach up to some shelves. Most accessible were the three accordion files on the top shelf. I grabbed the closest one, pale blue and thick. We expanded the elastic band that held it closed, flipped open the flap, and found a stack of miscellaneous papers in need of sorting. Right in the very front were three cassette tapes that, out of curiosity, we removed from the file.

Jack quickly discovered that these tapes contained recordings of five meetings with Dr. Provisor at various junctures in Aimee's treatment between 1988 and 1993. There had been several other meetings over the years, all important, but somehow these were the ones that had gotten recorded. I remembered our concern about missing something important from these discussions and our decision for Jack to make recordings. We could only absorb so much at those times. Fortunately we were working with a physician who was not intimidated by our request.

Sometimes our whole family attended these meetings, other times parents and Aimee, rarely just parents. The girls were more witnesses than participants. Aimee's processing and talking came later in the van or at home. Molly listened. I remember vividly when, as an eight-year-old she said to me, "I don't understand all that goes on in those meetings, but I sure am glad I'm there."

Jack and I did not listen to every tape afterwards; the girls did not listen to any of them. They had been stored away for twenty to twenty-six years when we found them. As audiotape recordings of several important turning points in Aimee's treatment, they offered another portal for connecting to our family's experience during those treatment years. Jack digitized the tapes the following week and sent them to both Molly and me. He said that he did not want to, could not, listen to them. Molly and I decided to give them a try. Her decision was more innocent than mine. I remembered the gravity of the content, some of the exact words. She was a young child during those years and hadn't been at every meeting.

Wandering in the Wilderness

We agreed upon a schedule to listen to one meeting a day over about a week's time. Since Molly was in Brooklyn and I in West Lafayette, we decided to listen separately whenever we could during the day, and then discuss the meeting tape of the day by phone in the evening. I had a strong sense that these recordings would evoke the emotions and confusion of the times when they were recorded. My feeling was that if I was going to listen to them, I needed the structure of processing them with Molly. She felt the same way. I cried my way through each tape each day as I listened and girded myself emotionally to talk in the evening.

These recordings were made over an almost six-year time span. Below are brief excerpts from each of them introduced by a short description of the context and followed by general reactions from Molly and/or me. Initials for each participant are used after the first use of his or her name.

February 1988: two years post initial diagnosis

The earliest and most optimistic of these recordings occurred two years into Aimee's initial treatment with five more months until its completion. Jack had taken both of the girls down to Indianapolis for Aimee's appointment; I had to work that day. He also wanted to talk to Dr. Provisor about possible travel with Aimee. Jack made this first recording so that I could hear their conversation. The girls were eight and four years old.

> **Jack**: Testing 1-2-3-4. Let's talk a little bit girls. Hello, Mom. Tell Mom where you are.
> **Aimee**: Mom?
> **J:** Yes. Well this recording is for Mom so she'll . . .
> **Molly**: I'm at Riley, Mommy.
> **A:** We're at Riley, Mom, in room six. I already got a blood test.
> **M:** And I have . . . there's a book here, and it's called
> **M & A in unison**: *Turtle Magazine*
> **A:** We found it with the books in the room.
> **M:** Yah. In room six where we are.
> **A:** And when Dr. Provisor walked by and I was getting my temperature, or whatever, something like that, he

goes, "Urrrr." (Laughter from both girls) But Molly was out in the playroom then.
M: Yeah.

Soon after, Aimee's physician entered the room and was admiring the girls' art work.

Dr. Provisor: Aimee and Molly, where did you make these? Out in the waiting room?
A & M: Yeah.
Dr. P: These are beautiful things, Jack.
J: Well, they're real artists, aren't they?

Later Jack and Dr. Provisor talked together by themselves.

Dr. P: Her life hasn't changed that much. She's in school. She's lead a pretty darn normal existence. . . . Both you and Mary Jane have done an excellent job of not keeping Aimee in a cocoon, letting her live a very normal life. . . . Psychologically this is a very well put together child, sensitive, a little bit high strung in some ways, but a very well put together child. . . . Making life decisions is uncertain when we can't say to you that she's definitely cured from the disease. But you've been living with that veil for two years plus, and life goes on as you have demonstrated so wonderfully—and life will continue to go on.
J: I am of the opinion that we must proceed with life. One way we have managed to cope with this disease is that we're proceeding as if everything is going to turn out ok because I don't know how else to do it.
Dr. P: Well there is no other way to do it. . . . To paralyze one's entire life would be so defeating for the person who has this problem, for Aimee. If you hadn't proceeded the way you have, she could have become an emotionally disturbed child. And she's not at all

As I listened to and thought about this conversation so many years later, I extended these remarks to Molly's life. It was an optimistic time in treatment as Aimee headed into her last months of maintenance, a time of reduced medications before ending chemotherapy. It was heartwarming to hear the sweet voices of my daughters and the wisdom of these two men. Molly found this listening to be a sentimental introduction to the task we had assigned to ourselves.

May 1990: four months post first relapse

After Aimee's first relapse in 1990, our meetings shifted to debates about treatment options, none of which guaranteed a favorable outcome. All four of us had met with Dr. Provisor in January of 1990, the day after we learned of Aimee's relapse. She was ten years old and Molly six. That meeting hadn't been recorded. We were out of practice and in shock then. Its message had been very clear: Aimee's chances of long-term survival on chemotherapy were quite poor.

This May discussion, four months later and with parents only, included more clinical data and a reiteration and expansion of the earlier message. As I listened, I felt the heaviness of the issues, my utter sadness for Aimee, and our responsibility to understand every detail of what was said. The comfort of a collaborative approach helped to contain these feelings. Aimee's physician was a very bright man who had the ability to explain medical issues in clear, logical and humanistic terms while also acknowledging the imperfections of medical science and her unique characteristics as a pediatric cancer patient.

> **Dr. P**: I'm becoming more and more a believer in cytogenetics and what cytogenetics tell us. And cytogenetics is telling me that Aimee has a lousy clone of cells that statistically have a poor outlook. In other words, in remission now, but how long are we going to stay? Our Day 14 marrow in the middle of January, how many blasts did we have? 24%. That wasn't great. Two weeks later, her marrow was perfect on Day 28. But in looking at newly diagnosed leukemia cases, one of the big what we call "front-end prognostic features" seems to be: What is their marrow two weeks into therapy? We don't expect it to be a complete remission. But we expect there to be kind of nothing in there—a few little

lymphocytes, maybe a blast. She had 24% blasts. So I'm just trying to stack up all this information for you.

J: We're talking about this time around?

Dr. P: Yes, this time around, not back in January of 1986, but this year.

Mary Jane: I remember that clearly, two weeks in. It was obvious to me that Aimee's results were not great.

Dr. P: I was delighted when I got that 28-day marrow. It was perfect.... But in addition to her chromosomes, I'm faced with that 14-day marrow this time. One other thing, having nothing to do with chromosomes, nothing to do with response on Day 14, is the liver, her liver. The drugs are damaging her liver, putting it as bluntly as I can.

Later the conversation focused on bone marrow transplants.

Dr. P: So why even think of a marrow transplant? I guess, forgetting about match, mismatch, just the concept of marrow transplant appeals to me in some ways because if we could get through it, and that's an *if*, then I wouldn't give her any more chemotherapy afterwards. And yet, the best statistic that I think I could give you would be somewhere around 40-50%. However, I believe that with chemotherapy alone—I'm just laying it out for you; I'm not a prophet—the chance for a permanent situation where she is free of leukemia is very small. I think she stands a high probability of relapse. So what we're looking at here is a terrible thing to think of. As parents it's one thing; I don't know how you can think of all of this and make decisions. As a physician who hopes to be objective—which with her I find difficult to do—but I'm pretty objective. I really am. Here's a child that functions at a superior level. I mean, even when she's sick and in the hospital, she does more in one morning than most functioning children do in three days. She's an absolutely amazing individual. And what you do with a transplant is to interrupt that functioning. I'm just saying if she had a match, what we'd do, we'd take it. It's like putting all our eggs in one basket. And if it works, great! But if it doesn't, if there are complications of transplantation, it's a bad situation. And here you take a child who on May 15 is really functioning well, and she may not be functioning well on October 15. We don't know that for sure. And do you subject her to an all or nothing situation? This is a real dilemma, the most difficult problem with anything to do with transplantation. . . . And should or does Aimee have any role in this decision?

Dr. Provisor wanted us to make an informed decision. He recommended that we consult with professionals he knew at the University of Minnesota who were experts on pediatric bone marrow transplantation and get their input. Jack and I read all the research we were able to find and spent hours discussing it together. When school was out, we headed to Minneapolis.

After listening to this recording, Molly said that she was shocked to hear how explicitly all this information had been spelled out in 1990 and to realize that she did not know about Aimee's prognosis in these terms. As a child, she had been present for the family discussion with Dr. Provisor about her sister's dire situation just a few months earlier, on the day after Aimee's relapse was discovered. I was certain that there had been family follow-up discussion at home afterwards. With a constricted heart and churning stomach, I was realizing that hearing and discussing did not equal comprehension for a six-year-old. Of course not. How did I think it had?

"Mom, Dr. Provisor spells it all out very clearly here. You knew Aimee was going to die four years before it happened! How come no one ever told me my sister was going to die?"

"Oh, honey, you just don't get it," was my immediate first thought. I was so emotionally shut down that I couldn't speak this thought. I resented the naiveté of her question about a situation that was exceedingly complex and painful. What came into my mind next were words I had heard so often from my father: "Have faith, Mary Jane." He wasn't talking about faith in religious doctrine. He meant faith in the process of life, forces larger than ourselves, to work out difficulties and misunderstandings over time. I didn't attempt to answer Molly's question then.

After we hung up, I remembered the anguish of talking to Aimee at home about these tough choices, trying to support her emotionally and to help her understand what was difficult for us to comprehend. I don't think Jack and I knew how to translate this information to our younger child, and questioned whether it was even appropriate to try. We probably spoke to Molly in more general terms about her sister's illness and the trip we would make to talk to Dr. Provisor's friends.

June 1990: after bone marrow transplant consult

Shortly after returning from Minnesota, Aimee, Jack and I met with Dr. Provisor. We had made the decision not to fully rule out bone marrow transplant but to continue with chemotherapy for now—to wait, to see, to hope for treatment advances. Aimee did not have a related match. An unrelated match was riskier according to our reading of the literature but was considered her best available transplant possibility. Quality of life issues weighed heavily here: "Q of L" for Aimee primarily but also for Molly, and for our nuclear and extended families. Dr. Provisor did not shy away from discussing this topic and had conditioned us early on to consider it in our decision-making process.

MJ: We've been talking a lot with Aimee. I think she needs to hear more. . .
J: We've had two lengthy talks with Aimee.
Dr. P: That letter where you summarize what you and Jack think after your trip to Minnesota and reading a lot of research, Mary Jane. I read that, and you have succinctly summarized the options and the pluses and minuses of each option. The way I look at it, I agree that if we had an allogeneic donor, if Molly were a match, I might think differently. I'm not sure, but I might. . . . The options of either autologous or this unrelated marrow donor situation to me are not as promising as I'd like them to be. They don't have an offer of success *at this point* in her course.
So I would like to do what you suggested. I think it's best to proceed on the course we're doing. Let's say, for instance, we get through two more years of this and we're doing well, go off of therapy. That's fine; I

wouldn't do a thing. No one has the answers that you want. This one question about Aimee's chromosomes—what we do know is that those chromosomes are associated with a high risk of relapse, not necessarily 100% per case. . . . So to find out how children with Aimee's cytogenetics do with bone marrow transplant, I could inquire but it's not going to be . . .
J: We asked them about that. They said it was an academic question.
MJ: They didn't know. They had no idea.

In the evening when adult Molly and I talked about this recording, I realized that she was digging much more deeply into the history of Aimee's disease through the words of the physician most intimately connected to those years. Both through his words and her own follow-up reading, Molly was learning more about chemotherapy agents and their effects on the body, the risks and complexity of bone marrow transplant, and the difficulty of treatment decisions without full information or assurances of success. She began asking me questions about Aimee's chemotherapy drugs and treatment protocols, questions I had never heard from her before. I had been waiting for them for years. I felt like Molly was starting to more fully own her sister's experience with leukemia by examining its specifics at a much deeper level.

July 1992: one day after second relapse

Aimee and I had been down to Dr. Provisor's the day before this meeting. That appointment was supposed to be the end of her first-relapse treatment protocol. Tragically it was the discovery of a second relapse. He wanted us to return the next afternoon with the rest of our family for a 'Security Council' meeting. Molly's young voice opened this recording with a sweet eight-year-old "Hi!" full of innocence and openness. It was an exhausting, almost two hour meeting—full of medication names, treatment details and new challenges for all of us, primarily for twelve-year-old Aimee. Her doctor and his two skilled and trusted nurses sat with us, trying to prepare us. As always, these meetings were respectful and surprisingly included some humor.

> **Dr. P**: We all decided back in the spring of 1990 that we would cross our fingers and take our chances with chemotherapy. Even with the alterations in liver functions, I would submit to you that the past two plus years have not been bad years.
> **MJ**: They've been great years.
> **Dr. P**: I think my colleagues both in and out of bone marrow transplantation would say that, had we transplanted Aimee, we would not have had such a smooth course, and number two, I'd say there would still be just as great a chance that she could have relapsed at this point. . . . But now with a second relapse, a bone marrow transplant with an unrelated match actually offers Aimee a better chance for extending life than chemotherapy does. Personally I think we'll be headed to a transplant situation in 6–8 months.

After an intricate description of each drug involved in a very aggressive European chemotherapy protocol ("a sledge hammer with a sponge") to hopefully get Aimee into remission, the nurses showed us two possible central lines to consider, both requiring surgery for insertion. Either of them could help streamline procedures for frequent IV drugs, blood draws, and possibly even liquid nutrition. At first Aimee didn't know what she wanted to do treatment-wise, but as time filled with questions and explanations went by that afternoon, we all came around to choosing the proposed treatment plan.

> **Dr. P**: We are going to put her in the hospital to start chemotherapy. She'll be in the hospital for a minimum of five or six days, and . . .
> **J**: But we could do the central line surgery then, with that first hospitalization. That would be most efficient, to just go ahead then.
> **Dr. P**: You know, sometimes you really do crystalize everything, Jack. I agree!
> **J**: I would say that with Aimee (pause) we always underestimate her resiliency, how well she will do. That's why I want the device that will give her the most freedom because I believe Aimee will want it, need it.

Dr. P: Your daughter is a mover. Yes, the least disruptive to the Aimee Gandour lifestyle would be the subcutaneous port.

Aimee's recall about details of past treatment protocols prompted him to kiddingly call her "a hematologist in training." Molly appeared to be listening intently particularly during the hands-on central line demonstration. Dr. Provisor wanted to move her out of the draft of the air conditioner at one point and asked her and us if he could sit next to her. Of course.

Our next task was to make a decision about when to start this treatment protocol within the next six days.

> **MJ**: Well, I think we need a couple of days. I don't know. We can talk about it. I don't know how the rest of you are doing, but I don't do real well with this stuff at first. It has to sink in a little bit.
> **Dr. P**: Do you want to talk about this without me in the room—about your timing? Because I am willing to do almost anything you want. I just need advance warning. If you have things you want to talk about or you think one thing and the king thinks another and the crown princesses have their ideas. I don't think you need me around to have a discussion.
> **MJ**: That's true.
> **Dr. P**: I can step out and wait. Why don't I do that, if it's ok with you?
> **J**: Yes, then we . . .
> **Dr. P**: If I hear fistfighting, I will come in. (door shuts)
> **MJ**: I think what matters most is how Aimee feels about when to get started. I was thinking there are 4-H projects and the strings concert. Maybe Friday. I don't know. . . . I feel like I need at least a day.
> **J**: I'm just thinking about the leukemia in her body. What do you think Aimee?
> **A**: Well, I mean, if it's not going to make any difference, I kind of want to do the strings concert.
> **J**: Well, maybe Friday? I wouldn't want to wait any longer

> **Aimee:** Well, I mean, if it's going to make a difference, then we'll go sooner.
> **MJ**: Of course, we will.

Our conversation that night after listening to this tape was heavy and gloomy. We both acknowledged how somber it sounded, how emotionally draining the listening had been. These events were vivid in both of our minds. Molly said that even as an eight-year-old, she sensed a clear demarcation between her sweet childhood and a much darker, more challenging time of life after this meeting. She commented that Aimee's voice sounded "so small." Gone was the loud, animated chit-chat of the little artists of 1988. Molly had more insight into what this day meant in her life than I did at the time and for years afterwards. Her sister's disease had become more real for her in July of 1992, and was becoming even more heartfelt so many years later.

October 1993: one day after third relapse

This last recording was made a year and three months later, the day after Grandma Gandour had gone down to Aimee's appointment with us, only to learn the devastating news that she had relapsed a third time. Dr. Provisor wanted to see Aimee, Jack and me the next day. Molly was in her fourth-grade classroom that afternoon, and Grandma was on hand for her after school. Molly had just turned ten; Aimee was soon to be fourteen.

> **Dr. P**: Aimee is aware of the results of the bone marrow yesterday? You were so groggy from the Versed when I was talking, and I think you were asleep. . . . Basically you're feeling fine; your examination was fine; your marrow has 86% lymphoblasts. . . . There's no doubt that it's a relapse.

At this point, we had done everything as far as traditional therapy was concerned. Since Aimee's exam the day before, Dr. Provisor had learned about an NIH and FDA-approved investigational drug study that targeted cancer cells with a particular marker that her leukemic cells happened to have. He had talked with the physician who was the principal investigator and suggested that we also talk with him.

Dr. P: The first thing he asked me about was the condition of the patient. I said A+ like her grades, because it is. Even with three relapses of leukemia, she is pretty functional.

He described the possibility of investigational drugs in more detail. The amount of information was overwhelming to all of us, especially Aimee, who sat silently listening. She didn't ask any questions.

J: If we were to do nothing,
Dr. P: That's an option.
J: what's the course you would predict?
Dr. P: Within two weeks, she would probably need some form of blood transfusion, platelets. Her immune system, her ability to fight infection, would be affected. . . Maybe a month. . . .This is a full blown leukemic relapse! . . . My advice is for you to talk to this physician. . . . If we decide to do it, I'd like to have her there within a week. It takes a certain amount of time to get it through their institutional review, to get her eligible. . . . I'm saying this might be an option. If the three of you decide right now, I don't want to do it, you are not going to incur my wrath at all. I can understand that fully.
J: Your job is to present the options.
Dr. P: Absolutely.

Later I brought up the topic of no treatment again.

MJ: I want to understand more about what the course of events is for Aimee if we don't do anything.
Dr. P: It's a very hard thing. . . . I'm saying. . .
MJ: I mean, let's get it out!
Dr. P: OK, if her platelets go down, we can deal with that. If you are worried about overwhelming bleeding, that is less of a problem. The major problem for Aimee will be an overwhelming bacterial or fungal infection.

Aimee doesn't have the white cells to fight it—lymphocytes and neutrophils: ANC, AGC and ALC, she doesn't have those.

MJ: So she's really susceptible to infection. What would she be like in terms of what she can do, how she would function?

Nurse: Joint pain, cold and congestion, respiratory infection...

Dr. P: Her marrow is perking along very well. It wasn't difficult to get marrow from her yesterday. Bone pain from leukemia is bone marrow pain. And her relapses, Mary Jane, did not have that feature. We've picked them up relatively quickly and started her on therapy which has been fairly effective in reducing the number of leukemic cells. The last one took us longer until we got into a remission...

MJ: How quickly could Aimee's cancer cells go from 86% to 100% and how different would she be?

Dr. P: My sense with Aimee is that even when she's bad, she's still pretty good.... That's a terrible way to put it.

Jack and I knew that we had a lot to learn here and to decide upon—quickly. The tape went from our discussion with Dr. Provisor to our conversation with this investigator. Most likely there was an unrecorded gap in between when Jack, Aimee and I were formulating questions and writing them down. The entire line of questioning from this conference call is recorded on this final tape, including questions like the following: What do you have in writing about this protocol that we can read? How many kids have you tried on this drug who are in Aimee's situation and what kind of results have you had? What was the aftermath for children who did not achieve a remission? What are the most common side effects?

Molly and I both found it difficult to listen to this last recording knowing that we had chosen this treatment, and it had not worked. We knew that this physician-researcher had done all he possibly could for Aimee. Only in this listening did we realize the possible connection between the investigational drug and the fungal pneumonia that Aimee developed in December. Another possible connection, a positive one, was Aimee's unexplained miraculous remission in January of 1994, which allowed a period of grace before her death in March. Could it have been a delayed reaction to this treatment?

Initially the specifics of these taped meetings were not my primary concern, but rather the fact that they had taken place, often within a family context, and had been recorded. It was Molly who wanted to carefully review the medical details. I continued to be surprised by how little she seemed to know about her sister's illness. I reminded myself that she had been four to barely ten years-old when these recordings had been made. She could not possibly have understood or internalized the particulars of her sister's treatment then.

After we finished listening to the tapes, Molly continued to ask questions. What was the chromosomal makeup of her sister's cancer cells? What exactly was the difference between an autologous and allogeneic bone marrow transplant? Specifically how had chemotherapy affected Aimee's liver? Her questions became deeper as the weeks went on. As an adult, she was reviewing data that she didn't even know existed, trying to clarify more about her sister's disease. At last, she was using her adult cognitive skills to explore the years before the trauma of her sister's death.

I felt a sense of relief that she was asking so many questions. As a mother, I had paid compulsive attention to every detail of Aimee's treatment, documenting dates, symptoms, blood tests, medications, physician instructions. Most days Jack and I openly discussed some aspect of her care. Aimee herself, particularly after her first relapse, became very knowledgeable about her treatment—the names of drugs, how they were administered, what they felt like in her body, when side effects would hit the hardest, which drugs were inpatient and outpatient. I somehow assumed that Molly knew this information too, as if she had learned it by osmosis simply living in our home, observing Aimee, listening to our discussions and explanations, and attending several of these meetings. It was a form of adult magical thinking on my part.

As familiar as I had been with treatment so many years ago, I needed to go back and refresh my mind, so that I could be sure I was giving Molly accurate information. I had barely touched Aimee's medical information since her death. It was too emotional to go near it. I revisited the blue accordion file plus the red one and brown one that stood next to it. I also pulled file folders out of my desk drawers, the ones color-coded purple for Aimee. In these places, I found treatment protocols, medical records, lists of care instructions, documentation of symptoms, and results of blood tests lined up next to each other across months, ultimately years.

In this process, I was pulled back into the compelling world of clinical information that for years had helped to give me a sense of control. It was something to organize and master, a place to feel some intellectual challenge, to be given a second chance at understanding by simply rereading, or to correct a number easily by erasing and rewriting. It was a solitary pursuit that I would disappear into from time to time. I had just enough background in the sciences to feel comfortable examining data. Reading medical articles and book chapters felt affirming and satisfying despite their difficulty. I didn't fully understand this world of medical information, but I liked trying to understand it. This pursuit helped to ground me.

Certainly the recordings were the most engrossing of all the medical resources because they were live and felt real in the listening. However, the specifics, the numbers, the terminology, were in the medical records. I was spellbound by a series of letters from Aimee's hematologist to her pediatrician over the years of her treatment. I cried as I read the medicalized version of my daughter but also felt reassured to know how much was being monitored and communicated about her physical state. I conceptualized at a deeper level about the larger clinical picture of what had happened to Aimee over the years.

I made copies of these letters for Molly. I started to accept how little of this medical information she had comprehended as a child. She read everything I sent her and used it as a springboard to seek out more targeted information about leukemia. I felt grateful that Jack had made these recordings and that Molly and I had listened to them. I felt an enhanced optimism about her journey and felt my love for Aimee in a calmer, less distracted way.

Over this time of listening and exploring, I developed a strong sense that, for Molly, this time provided a link to her childhood emotional experience during Aimee's illness. The dynamic of knowing and not knowing, never fully recognized or labeled as such, had played out across most of her life, all of our lives in one way or another.

The diaries had documented day to day events and changes in our girls' lives at a personal level, both when medical treatment was a factor and when it was not. The recorded conversations from treatment turning points overlapped with both daily life and the written medical information. In combination with our therapeutic work, these wilderness resources created an enlarged picture of our family's experience.

I listened to the recordings a couple more times and typed full transcripts of the last two. When I finally let go of them, it was with the feeling that Jack and I had done the best we could at the time for Aimee and Molly. Everyone involved had. I felt a lot of respect for us as devoted investigative partners, as communicators with Aimee's physicians, and as loving parents to our daughters. All the medical information is back where I found it, with that heavy table again blocking access to the closet with the accordion files.

Christmas boxes in the garage

Nativity Resurrection

One Christmas season
A struggling young woman found life.
Multifaceted expressions of love
Lifted her up,
Healed her,
Allowed her more time
To experience and learn about
The God within her
And within the dear people connected to her
Who collectively gave her life.

Mary Jane Gandour
January, 1994
Two months before Aimee's death

Christmas boxes with a variety of labels—Ornaments, Lights, Nativity Set, Angels, Fireplace, and many more—were stacked in our garage, right next to the green bins of Aimee memorabilia. Even in warm weather, even in their unopened state, these boxes could easily pull me into the magic and confusion of the holidays. They became another resource for wilderness exploration, not the boxed-up objects themselves but the history they had witnessed with our family

We had developed holiday traditions over the years. After listening to holiday music all morning and preparing our 'sleigh', we drove around midday on Christmas Eve delivering cookies and gifts to friends. In the evening, we attended Christmas Eve Mass followed by a dinner celebrating family ethnicities: Lebanese soup and Irish soda bread, as well as a fruit salad shaped like a wreath incorporating as many red and green fruits as I could find. In the girls' younger years, we put out cookies for Santa, carrots for the reindeer and a little note welcoming them. We always read *Twas the Night before Christmas* and later added *The Polar Express*. Each of us opened one present from a relative.

On Christmas morning, the girls always woke up before us but weren't allowed to go downstairs until both Mom and Dad were up. We loved watching their faces as they enthusiastically examined their gifts and reacted warmly and gratefully to what they found. Santa always left a one-page letter for them, mostly philosophical in nature, which we read together before digging into stockings.

We opened presents, explored the gifts that had arrived, laughed, ate, listened to Christmas music, enjoyed the fire in the fireplace, played new games, and talked to relatives far and wide. Everyone helped out with dinner preparations, and at some point we all got cleaned up. We didn't have other people over because many of our friends were out of town or had their own family traditions that shaped the day. Thanksgiving was our grand holiday away with extended family in Pittsburgh. Christmas was our own most years. There was an absolute magic to the bubble we created for our little family here at home on this day, which we all cherished deeply. There was no other time quite like it in the year. We topped the evening off by driving around in the dark and cold looking at Christmas lights in nearby neighborhoods.

We had our last Christmas with Aimee in 1993.

Earlier that December when we were making decisions about surgery, Aimee asked her infectious disease doctor a long sequence of questions. At the end, she looked him straight in the eyes and inquired, "If I don't have this surgery, how many days do I have?"

He answered, "Maybe as few as three."

Then with tears streaming down her face, she asked, "If I have this surgery, will I make it to Christmas?"

He answered that he couldn't say for sure, but he thought it was a good possibility, and probably more time.

"I want to have this surgery!" was her response.

Our family problem solving process brought us to a peaceful conclusion that, yes, we would do this surgery.

A few days before Christmas, we brought Aimee home with hospice care. A large intergenerational group of friends greeted her in our front yard, holding lighted candles and singing holiday carols. She waved gently and smiled for the few minutes her energy allowed.

We decorated our tree together. We made it to Christmas Eve Mass, Aimee tethered to an oxygen tank. We had our usual dinner and rituals. Early the next morning, a hospice nurse came to administer several medications before anything else could happen. Getting Aimee and her oxygen tank down the steps on Christmas morning required our support and assistance. It was a cooperative family task. I had very little time to shop that year and kidded about our Methodist Hospital Gift Shop Christmas. We hardly noticed because so many relatives and friends had been so generous to us, and, much more importantly, Aimee was alive, we were at home, and our family was together. We moved and reacted in a more deliberate, less spontaneous manner that Christmas, unconsciously pacing ourselves to mirror Aimee's slowed down functioning. Molly helped her sister move about and brought her everything from food to a portable telephone.

In the days afterwards, again supported by her sister, Aimee made belated Christmas presents for her grandparents, aunts, uncles and cousins during days punctuated with taking medications and trying to eat. In the crafts room, she wove baskets, tie-dyed shirts, beaded necklaces, decorated hats, and painted boxes. There was a sense of urgency and determination to this creative mission that went on for days. She wrapped these gifts, and we mailed them to Mississippi, Florida, California, Pennsylvania, Virginia. In the autumn she had managed to finish making boxer shorts for her friends at the hospital. When Aimee felt a little stronger, there was a belated holiday gift exchange with them.

I vividly remember a Saturday morning at the end of those holidays when Molly and I were in the bathroom curling her hair into ringlets for her angel role in Lafayette Ballet's *The Nutcracker*. Right across the hall from us, a hospice nurse was giving Aimee a blood transfusion in her bedroom. The juxtaposition of these two scenes captured something unnerving about life moving on and life slowing down. The next day Aimee managed to make it to her sister's matinee show. Molly performed beautifully. Our family went to the reception at the ballet school afterwards. We came home and started Aimee's antifungal IV infusion. Seeing refrigerator shelves filled with bags and syringes of medication was unavoidable as dinner preparations began.

After Aimee died in March 1994, our family had a difficult time figuring out what to do with Christmas. For the first two years, we didn't deviate much from our traditions; I don't think we wanted to. It seemed important to preserve what we could for Molly. I had heard of mothers refusing to put up trees or to buy gifts after a death. I knew that ignoring traditional aspects of Christmas was not the way I wanted to proceed. Our one variation was to read *Twas the Night before Christmas* not from a book but from recycled paper, the blank side of one of Jack's old manuscripts, where Aimee had stamped out the whole story. She started it on Christmas Eve of 1989, and, with her father's encouragement, finished it in two more sittings just before Christmas 1990. There was not a mistake in its thirty pages. Jack had it laminated after Aimee died and kept it in a manila envelope with family scrapbooks. Reading the story from these pages brought Aimee closer to us, knowing that she had stamped its words right in the crafts room downstairs.

Wandering in the Wilderness

I worked at finding other ways to remember Aimee on Christmas across the years. I bought a Christmas wreath, usually to support a high school fundraiser, and we'd take it to the cemetery, often in the snow. I used holiday napkin rings that Aimee had made the year before she died and always included ornaments from across the girls' preschool and elementary years on our tree. I wore a Christmas apron Aimee had painted for me. We lit a candle for her at Christmas dinner and remembered her in our grace. My efforts to talk about Aimee on this day met with silence. On this holiday of holidays, I didn't recognize that my husband and daughter's grief was expressed differently than mine and that Molly was growing beyond our earlier versions of Christmas.

In 1999 when Molly was fifteen and in the ninth grade, she wrote a nine-page essay for her English class called *Christmas Times*, which she gave to Jack as a Christmas gift. The complete text is in Appendix E. It described our Christmas rituals, how they changed after her sister died, and how it felt to Molly in the years that followed:

> *"It's funny how we can mark time, our state of mind, and our former levels of maturity by holidays. Every year when Christmas rolls around, it's time to look back on all past Christmases and just remember. The story of my Christmases tells so much. . . . She spent that entire Christmas with oxygen tubes in her nose. At the time, it didn't seem like that big of a deal to me. I had lived with her sickness as long as I could recall. Looking back, though, it's amazing that she smiled, laughed, and acted as if it were just another Christmas. I hardly realized that anything was different, for her smile gave me courage. . . . But Christmases go on and keep us connected and grounded in our past. The magic of Christmas is that it is always there, a break from normal life, a time to just relax and give and receive. Christmas is a reminder that life goes on."*

Heart Work

We all cried when Jack read it aloud to us. This tradition continued through Molly's high school years after which I found it too heartbreaking to hear. I asked that he not read it to us, in retrospect such a denial of exactly what I thought I had been hoping for—other rituals from Jack and Molly. I hadn't been able to grasp that truth at the time.

During 2011, the year following our family therapy in Indiana, Molly worked long hours in Manhattan as a film editor. We occasionally talked about possible changes for Christmas without coming to any conclusions. We saw Molly at least once a month across that year—at everything from a play in memory of Jack's mother in Miami to cousins' weddings in Istanbul, Turkey, and Portland, Oregon. We had traveled to New York and she to West Lafayette. Molly wasn't sure about her plans for Christmas; she seemed physically and emotionally exhausted when we saw her at Thanksgiving. We didn't pressure her.

Jack and I began to prepare ourselves for the possibility that, for the first time, Molly would not be with us for Christmas. The longer she didn't disclose her plans, the more certain we were that she wasn't coming. And we were right. She decided to stay in New York and celebrate with her boyfriend's family. Molly said she needed to rest and regroup despite feeling homesick and knowing she'd miss us. Phone calls and emails built understanding about her decision. We all openly acknowledged that we'd miss each other. She suggested that a year apart could be a good opportunity to clarify what our holiday time meant to us, what we wanted it to be. She asked for my cookie exchange recipe but was also thinking about baking biscotti. I called her after trimming our tree to tell her that, for the first time, I hadn't put every ornament on the tree, and it still looked gorgeous. She laughed.

As Christmas drew near, Jack and I felt sad. He was the one to utter the word "sad" one evening. As we were talking, he started to cry and went upstairs. In a few minutes, he came back down, composed. He said he missed Molly and missed Aimee and missed our family being together. He said that it was so much more fun when the girls were little, and Aimee was alive. I told him I shared those feelings. We reminisced about Christmas Eves and Christmas Days Past—including the first year that the girls went up to the altar together, hand in hand, to hear the Christmas story with the other children at Mass

Later I read my journal entries from Christmas the year before. The words were so raw. I had forgotten how painful it all had been. Not having Molly at home this year made sense and felt like an investment in something better for the future. The constriction in my chest started to soften. We read *Twas the Night before Christmas* in the darkness of early Christmas morning, noticing how Aimee had dated each of her three stamping sessions. Jack then read Molly's *Christmas Times* aloud, and we re-appreciated its imagery, complexity and wisdom. We shed tears of gratitude for both of our daughters.

There were texts and phone calls from Molly at poignant times all during the holiday week. She had missed us, but seemed peaceful with her decision to stay in New York. She said she had great childhood memories of Christmas, a family and community time for us.

This contact with her was part of a larger holiday season for us. It included a new friend's German Solstice party, the annual cookie exchange with my longstanding 'mom' friends, an evening with our neighbors, lunch with my former colleagues, buying presents, cooking a lot, going to church, a Christmas feast with friends, an open house where several of Aimee's friends showed up, celebrating our wedding anniversary, and a New Year's Eve party with close friends. I was relieved when the holidays were over, knowing that we had survived. I longed for both of our daughters and redefinition of future Christmases.

Molly joined us for the next two holiday seasons on her own initiative and with chats around Thanksgiving about what we might do. She sought input from her cousin Rochelle and Aimee's friend Erin. We changed some menus and spent Christmas Eve and Christmas night in more social ways. Molly baked biscotti for us. We talked calmly about our relationships. The house was reasonably but not elaborately decorated. The tree was in a slightly different place. One night we were snowed in with soup, bread and Scrabble, relaxed and kidding around with each other. Another year we attended the funeral of the girls' pediatrician, Wendell Riggs, MD on Christmas Eve with gratitude for his patient persistence with Aimee's early symptoms. The calm of these

Heart Work

Christmases gave us a sense that Aimee was participating with us. We didn't have to summon her. She was there in our connectedness.

In the fall of 2014 Molly started a graduate program in film at NYU. The program was intense, and her semester didn't end until close to Christmas. Jack and I both thought about spending the holidays in New York. When we mentioned this possibility to Molly, she was thrilled. We looked into flights, hotel options, opera tickets, restaurants, what we might do together. The enthusiasm was contagious as we all anticipated the holidays together. Before we left, there was the joy of my annual cookie exchange, a Hanukkah gathering, a holiday concert, and the Solstice party. Part of our holidays was comfortably at home.

In New York we met Molly, the competent adult on her own turf. Our commitment to a redefined holiday season made the situation feel unique in our family history. Molly seemed more committed to a relationship, a profession, her family. We saw pictures and artwork in her apartment that were reminders of her childhood and sister. She cooked a lavish birthday dinner for me, introduced us to interesting restaurants, and advised us about transportation options. We had time together as well as stretches for our own exploration. Christmas Eve with her boyfriend's family was relaxed and fun. We found a sweet urban church hidden away on a Brooklyn side street for Christmas Mass.

The day after we came home, we attended an open house at the Pines Farm where Aimee had often spent precious childhood time. Her friend Erin's family had owned this farm for generations. For us, our daughter felt more present at the farm that evening than at any other time we had been there since her death. I think that letting go of the past and focusing on the present allowed Aimee back in, made the holidays more as they would have been, had she still been alive.

What started out as an experiment ended up as a revelation of increasing truth: Aimee will show up regardless of where or how we celebrate the Christmas season

I packed up what decorations I had taken out that year, not too many, and Jack took the boxes back out to the garage, as he always has after the holidays.

Chapter Four ~ *Returning with the Questions*

> *We look with uncertainty*
> *beyond the old choices for*
> *clear-cut answers*
> *to a softer, more permeable aliveness*
> *which is every moment*
> *at the brink of death;*
> *for something new is being born in us*
> *if we but let it.*
> *We stand in a new doorway,*
> *awaiting that which comes . . .*
> *daring to be human creatures,*
> *vulnerable to the beauty of existence.*
> *Learning to love.*
>
> Anne Hillman, *Awakening the Energies of Love*

> *I would like to beg you, dear Sir, as well as I can, to have patience with everything unresolved in your heart and to try to love the <u>questions themselves</u> as if they were locked rooms or books written in a very foreign language. Don't search for the answers, which could not be given to you now, because you would not be able to live them. And the point is, to live everything. <u>Live</u> the questions now. Perhaps then, someday far in the future, you will gradually, without even noticing it, live your way into the answer.*
>
> Rainer Maria Rilke, *Letters to a Young Poet*

Mine was an interior pilgrimage, a journey of the heart. I returned home in fits and starts. The Wilderness was dense and evoked challenging emotions from me. But it was also strangely absorbing and gratifying. I wandered there for years investigating and processing what had happened during our family work together, as well as during our daughters' childhoods, Aimee's illness, and those lonely years after her death. I tentatively returned early as a psychotherapist doing her work and later more solidly as a retired person writing to relearn her life.

Heart Work

Pilgrimage requires courage, risk and vulnerability at the outset and probably just as much at the return. Over and over, we surrender our control during the journey. Pilgrimage does not inspire us to change so much as it changes us. Simply yearning for self-transformation through the grace of pilgrimage holds no guarantees. Sometimes our change is not planned or voluntary. It may not be what we were anticipating. Often it is irreversible. We bring this experience back into our lives. The return from a pilgrimage can feel like the beginning of another pilgrimage, but this time with enhanced gifts of compassion, humility and openness.[1]

Returning home requires adjustment. There are basic questions that we live with and, if we are fortunate, learn to love: What difference does it make that I have made this inner journey? What did pilgrimage teach me? How am I different? How will home be different? How are the important relationships in my life changed by this experience?

I came home asking more about dying children and their siblings, and how our family survived Aimee's illness and death. I questioned and wanted to explore my unease with the dark side of life. Much of my attention gravitated to relationships within the family—questions, observations, curiosities. Themes of paradox, creativity, and hope swirled around within each of these topics.

Living with paradox is one of the most challenging tasks in life, one that defines our uniqueness as human beings.[2] It involves dwelling with seemingly contradictory points of view and finding a way to live between them, within a third solution that flows out of these contradictions. In our case, we lived between the "swaying tension"[3] of life and death in a third situation that emerged out of our struggle between the two. For years we managed to sustain these contradictions in ways I cannot fully explain, but this mystery of paradox underlies questions I have lived with since my return.

Our girls were described as creative before leukemia ever entered our lives. This early baseline predicted creativity as a major support in the years ahead. But what is the relationship between creativity and disease, pain, and life giving energy? After years of exploring this question, Kenzoburo Oe, Japanese novelist, Nobel Prize winner, and father of a handicapped son, concluded that "illness can spur creativity and that creativity can help us when we are ill."[4] Miriam Greenspan described creativity as "the great healer," and creative flow as "emotional surrender."[5] Creativity remains a splendid gift and theme in our lives, one beyond words.

The concept of hope continued to occupy my thoughts—what it means, where it fits in with serious illness, the heartening and uneasy feelings that can surround it. Initially what we called hope was wishing, focused on the future. With relapse, hope had more to do with the now. It became a way of seeing ourselves, of approaching the day, of seeking meaning and engagement in our lives. As Sherwin Newland wrote in *How We Die*: "The greatest dignity to be found in death is the dignity of the life that preceded it. . . . Hope resides in the meaning of what our lives have been."[6]

Death Talk

Free Again

Greetings from under the water! I am a silver molly fish. I used to be graceful and free, and I would swim and play joyously in the depths of the sea with all my other molly fish friends. I was happy, and food was always plentiful. I had the freedom to do whatever my heart desired whenever I wanted.

Then, one day, everything changed. I was swimming along and minding my own business when suddenly, out of the blue, I couldn't go any more. I flipped and maneuvered my fins, but something was blocking my way. I looked around me and saw a tightly woven net surrounding me. I swam all around and pushed against it, but there was no way out. I was suddenly lifted up and the next thing I knew, I was in a bucket of water with a whole bunch of other fish like me. The bucket was on a massive ship that sailed back to some huge port city. Strange men began tossing me to each other. I was feeling very sick. Finally I was tossed onto a big truck and whisked away to a store. At first I was afraid I'd be sold in a supermarket and be eaten. I knew that wasn't possible, though, because I'm not a food fish. I was dumped into a tank of water with about ten other fish. I looked around from inside the tank which didn't give me a great view. I saw dogs, cats, gerbils and other strange creatures I knew nothing about. I figured I was in some kind of a pet store. I was very frightened because a rumor was going around that it was easy to die if you lived in a fish tank, because many people didn't take care of their fish and tanks properly. I had to figure out some way to escape.

Then, one day, I had a plan. I would not eat much, so that I would get really thin and lose my pretty colors. The pet store owners would get fed up because no one would want to buy me, and they'd take me back to the sea. I decided to carry out my plan. For months and months, which seemed like years and years, I didn't eat much when I was fed. I became very ugly and weak. I couldn't bear to look at my reflection in the side of the tank. I had to believe in myself and stick to my plan, though, because I really wanted to be free again.

A few days later, it happened. A small green net was stuck into the tank, and I was picked up in it. At first I was afraid someone was buying me, but then I was put in a bucket and loaded onto a truck. The truck whisked me away to some odd place. I was left there overnight, and it was dark, gloomy and cold. But then, the next day, I was put on a ship. The ship went out on the ocean, and I was dumped back in along with a bunch of other fish I assumed were also rejects. My plan had worked, and I was free again, and I could go back to being my usual carefree, beautiful, content self.

      Aimee Gandour
      August, 1993
      Seven months before she died
      Assignment: Be an animal and solve a problem

As an adult, Molly talked about how much of a shock Aimee's death was for her. She brought this topic up both during our phone interviews and later discussions of the Dr. Provisor tapes. In a hurt and resentful voice, she claimed that she didn't know that her sister was going to die, that we didn't tell her even though we knew. She felt cheated by that omission. At the time Molly made these assertions, I was shocked because I had assumed that she knew her sister was going to die. But after more than eight years and despite all that Jack and I knew about Aimee's disease, her death came as a shock *for us* as well, even though cognitively we knew for several years that it was highly likely to happen—sometime.

After empathy and tears for Molly, for all of us, and the passage of some weeks after her comments, my defensiveness took over. For years, Jack and I had felt good about our approach of including Molly in some of Aimee's treatment while at the same time trying not to overwhelm her with her sister's disease. We certainly *had* talked with her about leukemia using all of the recommended child materials and our own wits to explain as much as we could to her.

Molly had been included in a number of meetings with Aimee's doctor when the low probability of her sister's long term survival was discussed. I had assumed that she grasped this information from the words and mood of these meetings and our well-intentioned efforts at explanations afterwards. She had gone with her sister for chemotherapy multiple times and sat with her watching videos while Aimee's IV dripped toxic chemicals into her body. She had gone to cancer camp with her sister twice and been around other young people with this disease. We had driven as a family to the University of Minnesota to explore a bone marrow transplant and later had a huge bone marrow donor drive at the girls' elementary school. Over the years Molly had visited her sister in the hospital numerous times, stayed overnight there a few times and later at Ronald McDonald House. Our family had celebrated an Easter and New Year's Eve in the hospital because Aimee was too ill to be home. Molly had sat in surgery waiting rooms, seen her sister intubated afterwards, and written notes back and forth with Aimee until she was able to talk. She had flown to Minneapolis with Jack to visit Aimee and me during treatment with an investigational drug. Two months later she saw medical equipment in our house, IV bags and syringes in our refrigerator, and oxygen tank deliveries around

Christmas. During January, she saw her sister, weak at home, unable to go to school. As one therapist put it, "Death was in the air."

Had we uttered and dwelled upon the actual words "death" and "dying" in a direct conversation with Molly? Did we explicitly spell out that all she was observing was related to death? I don't think so.

As I anguished over this issue, an imaginary, sarcastic dialogue between me and Molly scrolled through my mind:

> Oh, Molly, life feels kind of normal today. Let's talk about how ill your sister is and that she is going to die.
> *When?*
> Well, we don't know. It could be next week or in a year or two or three.
> *Where will she die?*
> I don't know. Probably in the hospital or at home.
> *What will it be like when she dies?*
> I don't know. I've never been around a dying person. I don't know what it's like.
> *Do other brothers and sisters go through this?*
> Yes, but very little is written about it or has been communicated to us about it.
> *Should I worry about Aimee dying, like if we're home alone together some night? What should I do if she died while I was alone with her?*
> Oh, we'll hope that never comes up. We won't leave you alone with Aimee if we think she's going to die that night.
> *Are there things that I can do to help her not die? Should I worry that I could make her die in some way?*
> Oh, no, honey. Just keep being who you are with Aimee.

Of course, this dialogue is not how a talk would ever have gone, but it points out some of the confusing elements of such a conversation. Trying to figure out when and how to tell Molly her sister was going to die was not on my mind. I think I simply believed that, given all that she had witnessed and heard, Molly knew that Aimee was going to die. I don't remember questioning that belief. I wasn't trying to trick *anyone*, let alone Molly. Well, perhaps myself.

Molly was not unfamiliar with the concept of death. I have no idea how many times the girls and I read and talked about *Charlotte's Web* and *The Fall of Freddie the Leaf*. Molly's hamster Fur Ball died two years before Aimee's death, and we had full family funeral rituals next to a hemlock tree in our backyard. Jack assisted a very tearful Molly with digging the grave. The four of us stood in our coats, arms around each other, as Fur Ball was lowered into the ground in a small cardboard box. Aimee made a wooden grave marker for him. Molly later created a textured cutout rendering of Fur Ball alive in his cage and wrote an explanation about what had happened leading up to his death including a possible diagnosis.

The only truth that we could have offered Molly in the last four plus years of Aimee's life was that it was highly likely that her sister would die. What does a child between the ages of six to ten do with that statement? If a sibling didn't die over some length of time, would she doubt that it was ever going to happen? Would she be on edge waiting for it to happen? Would she feel guilty if she wanted to get it over with? Would she look forward to the attention she might get as an only child? Would she think that wanting it to be over was why the ill sibling died sooner than expected? Would she feel that she needed to search for ways to keep her ill brother or sister alive? Would she walk on eggshells all the time, afraid to express emotions for fear they could kill her ill sibling? Would she also want to die? Would she be afraid to ask for extra attention or snuggling because she thought the dying child needed it more? Would she pray intensely to God for her sibling to live and then feel like she wasn't a good enough person or didn't pray hard enough when the sibling died? Would most children keep these thoughts from parents if they were experiencing them? An affirmative to any of these questions seems possible for a child in Molly's age range at the time.

Having said all this, I wish that we had had a long and loving talk with the whole family about Aimee's death—a young person's version of *The Conversation* [7]—probably in late 1993 or early 1994. I wish that Jack, Molly and I had sat down with Aimee to talk about her life, what she meant to us, and to hear what we meant to her. I wish that we had talked about how she wanted to die, what she wanted her funeral and burial to be like. I think that such an exchange would have been good for all of us. Some guidance and empowerment would have helped us to do this. Aimee herself had not initiated a family talk about her death. Perhaps she intuitively knew that sometimes words can fail, can be so inadequate at capturing the mystery and beauty of life. Or she couldn't find the words to even begin this conversation. Or she was waiting for one of us to initiate this talk, probably her parents.

The other possibility is that Aimee's last months with us were exactly as she wanted them to be—hanging out, when we were able, in ways that we had so often enjoyed across her life span. Perhaps what meant the most to her was the simple and the ordinary. She was leaving the rest up to us because she trusted our judgment and didn't want to burden herself with such onerous decisions as she was preparing to transition out of the life she had known with our family. She had expressed her love to us in multiple ways across the years, as we had expressed ours to her. Our heart legacy was extraordinary.

I think that in the big picture, Molly saw her sister as her sister, looking beyond her disease and physical changes. Do all siblings with an ill brother or sister do this? Would we want to prevent them from doing this? There was something beautiful and pure about her ability to see Aimee that way, but in the long run, it was poor preparation for the loss of her sister. We were naïve about how little Molly consciously realized, and frankly more focused on our dying child. Aimee and I had had several conversations about death; her sister wasn't present for them. When I thought about those talks, I realized that they were usually when we were in dire straits, often in a hospital setting. We and all the loving people who helped us out may have done too well at keeping Molly's life going. Aimee herself probably participated in this process, doing all she could to keep her own life and our lives moving forward. All of us came from a place of love. Molly was the most disadvantaged person in the mix, not because she was not taken seriously or not loved, but rather because she was young and cared for the best that we and everyone else who loved her knew how.

During my reading in the wilderness, I also learned that feelings of betrayal are not unusual for well siblings.[8]

The most ideal situation for discussing death is probably not a telling time but rather an ongoing conversation gently talking to the well sibling(s) about what they are thinking and experiencing over time, and encouraging them to talk, draw or play out their feelings as a spring board for discussion. *I thought that was what we had been doing.*

Molly did a lot of spontaneous drawing and writing related to Aimee's illness, often quietly left on the kitchen table before she ran out to the school bus or presented as Aimee and I were walking out the door to drive to the hospital. She had little to say about them, probably because they were replacements for her lack of words to express what she was feeling.

Her most dramatic drawing, entitled *Fighting for Life*, was created five months, almost to the day, before Aimee died and very soon after we learned that the investigational drug was not working. A horse is swimming but starting to sink in exceedingly turbulent waters of blues, greens and black that take up at least half of the page. Three bolts of lightning are just in front or behind the horse. The sky is black with layers of bright sunset colors below it. I don't remember being fully aware of this powerful crayon drawing until I came across it in a file years after Aimee's death. Is it possible that we didn't discuss it when it was drawn?

Molly also created a series of four linoleum block prints of butterflies in her art class at school, two in the months just before Aimee's death and two in the months after her death. Jack and I didn't see these butterflies until they appeared as a composite piece in the spring school art show. If Molly's conscious mind didn't realize that her sister was dying, her unconscious mind certainly did.

Therese Rando's research demonstrated that parents who live with a child's chronic illness for a protracted period of time are particularly ill-prepared when death comes.[9] Could this be true, perhaps even more so, for children whose siblings die after a long illness, in this case one that lasted for as long as Molly could remember? Why would we expect more from the sibling, a child, a disadvantaged griever, than we would of ourselves? What in life truly prepares us for the loss of a child, a sister, a friend?

Normalcy and Compartmentalization

> *"You didn't know about my diagnosis these last two years, did you? If you had known, it would have changed your relationship with me. Don't you think?" He grinned and ruffled my hair. "You know what's given me the greatest pleasure in life? It's been our bungalow, the normalcy of it, the ordinariness of my waking, Almaz rattling in the kitchen, my work. My classes, my rounds with the senior students. Seeing you and Shiva at dinner, then going to sleep with my wife."... I want my days to be that way. I don't want everyone to stop being normal. You know what I mean? To have all that ruined."*
>
> *... He looked at me intently.... "A gift, if you like. Give me as many normal days as I can possibly have."*
>
> Abraham Verghese, *Cutting for Stone*

A belief in the power of living as a whole person is foundational to my life. Yet, I've been thinking a lot lately about the benefits of compartmentalization.

Courtney E. Martin, *On Being*

On the day of diagnosis in 1986, Dr. Provisor advised us to keep our lives as *normal* as possible. In the years ahead, this counsel became a guiding principal that shaped our approach to cancer and our daily lives. My interpretation of normal was living life, to the degree possible, in the way our family would be living it, had this disease not intruded.

Of course, life was anything but normal, but, in our efforts to maintain the ordinary, we held onto our lives at home, in the community, and with our extended families. We did this by showing up every day that we reasonably could in the world that surrounded us: home, school, work, activities, social events, lessons, church, performances, appointments, and so on. Over the years, we showed up lots more times than we did not. It was a gritty, striving kind of hope that kept us going—finding meaning and a sense of belonging in the midst of uncertainty.

Even in the abnormality of the hospital, Aimee attempted to create a regular life by doing homework, talking to her friends, working on numerous crafts. She set up a bead shop in her hospital room and made necklaces and bracelets for nurses. We often brought along our portable sewing machine so that Aimee could work on her latest sewing project like making boxer shorts as holiday gifts for her friends, each pair of a different fabric. Like two escapees, we'd often jump back into the car after her hospital check-in and before her medications were fully ready for infusion. We knew we could count on that time to focus on fabric at a nearby strip mall. Aimee's face softened as she scrutinized prints and colors, matching them with the personalities and interests of friends. Then at the video store nearby we searched, debated and laughed about selections for our weekend entertainment before we headed back from our stolen normalcy. The poisons would usually be poised to assault Aimee's body by then.

So where normal wasn't, we attempted to bring it in. It also came in the form of Molly visiting the hospital as often as we could arrange so that the routine of having a sibling nearby could continue in some form. A smiling Molly carried boxes and bags to her sister's bedside—markers of multiple sorts, construction paper, acrylic paints, brushes, gimp, hemp, cassette tapes, word games, and sometimes an unfinished project from the crafts room. The girls interacted with some of the chatter and laughter of home, always with imagination and creativity. Molly sometimes brought homework to do alongside Aimee as she was doing hers. We watched Purdue basketball games. We did an Easter egg hunt one spring and a birthday party for me one winter. We had Aimee's room fully decorated for Christmas during her long hospital stay the December before she died. We did this for Aimee. We did this for ourselves.

Heart Work

Home felt like a sanctuary after these hospital detours. There was a comfort in the normal—schedules, family food and meals, a familiar bedroom and bathroom, our own washer and dryer, friends coming over, trees outside the window. And all four of us being there together. Despite the fact that cancer had intruded into our lives, we each tried to do what we usually did—like playing a musical instrument, solving an interesting math problem, dancing with expression, completing a manuscript for publication, giving a talk in the community, or simply baking some cookies.

During the last year and a half of Aimee's life, we knew full well that life was not normal as time in the hospital increased dramatically. She was there for a reason—to kill cancer cells or to recover from the dangerous side effects of the latest efforts to kill cancer cells. Disease was right in front of our faces there, everywhere from the blue and white hospital gown to the IV pole with its bulging bags to the chart at the bottom of the bed detailing every observation and procedure. The only normative aspect of the hospital was that it was normal to be sick there.

How did our family make it through the years of Aimee's leukemia? Looking back, I wondered how we kept as much normalcy as we did for as long as we did. Of course, the loving family and friends who unflinchingly stuck with us through it all and our own motivation, determination and beliefs had plenty to do with it. But at a practical level, how did we shift in one day, for example, from the procedures of Aimee's medical appointment, to paying attention to Molly's soccer game, to monitoring side effects, to trying to have a nice meal together? What determined where our minds and priorities were at any given time?

For me, the most insightful observations about how a family lives with a child's illness come from Myra Bluebond-Langner, an anthropologist who has studied seriously ill children, dying children, and their families, looking at both acute lymphoblastic leukemia and cystic fibrosis. She observed that families who face the possible terminal illness of a child work hard to preserve as much normalcy in their lives as possible for as long as they can, sometimes redefining normalcy with new sets of circumstances. And by doing what normal children do, an ill child finds that she can impact how others see her, as well as how her family sees her, how people see her family, and how she sees herself.[10] Our family was less unique than I had thought.

Dr. Bluebond-Langner observed that around a year into treatment, parents started to use strategies she referred to as *Compartmentalization* of information about the disease and the child's condition. She described the process as follows: "Information is processed and sorted in such a way that particular kinds of information are kept from immediate awareness. Decisions, conscious or unconscious, are made about where various kinds of information will be stored in their minds."[11] In a broader sense, compartmentalization is a defense mechanism, a way that humans protect themselves from the full emotional brunt of particular situations or conflicting beliefs in their lives. Many people rely on defense mechanisms of various kinds; therapists are slow to challenge them. The rule of thumb is that a person better have something as good or better to replace it with, if he or she is trying to eliminate a defense mechanism.

She reported that parents in her study talked about how necessary sorting information was, both for their own sanity and for getting things done. It gave them some sense of control over the illness, daily life, and their thoughts. Some parents were able to hold differing views of the disease, sometimes within a single day or a few hours. For example, they may be concerned about a bothersome side effect at the doctor's office but later in the day find themselves fully enjoying their child's school musical. Even when a child's physical condition starts to deteriorate, thoughts about the terminal prognosis may lessen somewhat when the child is not acutely ill. I could identify with both sets of circumstances.

To better understand how compartmentalization might have been working in our lives, I tailored her ingenious file cabinet metaphor to our situation.[12] I pictured a large filing cabinet labeled *Childhood Leukemia* containing multiple folders such as Acute Lymphoblastic Leukemia, Prognosis, Treatment Protocols, Chemotherapy Side Effects, Healthcare Insurance, Relapse, Bone Marrow Transplant, Terminal Diagnosis. In this metaphor, parents keep certain folders more accessible than others at particular times. For example, at the beginning of treatment, Chemotherapy Side Effects and Healthcare Insurance may be right in front of the top file drawer while Relapse may be in the back of the bottom drawer. Any file could be retrieved at any time, but there is an attempt to keep those that might interfere with the current situation out of the way. With each hospitalization or relapse or remission, information is rearranged again.

During Aimee's first remission which lasted nearly four years, we never opened the Relapse, Bone Marrow Transplant, or Terminal Diagnosis folders. Our full expectation was that she was going to survive cancer-free. The folders we had looked at so frequently—Treatment Protocols and Side Effects of Chemotherapy—went into a bottom drawer at the end of her initial treatment. With her first relapse, these folders once again became of prime importance, and, along with Relapse and Bone Marrow Transplant, they moved to the front of the top drawer, the forefront of our parental concerns. Toward the end of her life, it took a long time for us to drag the Terminal Diagnosis folder to the top drawer and then more time to move it to the front.

Cognitive dissonance—our inability to hold two contradictory beliefs like life and death together at one time—and the intensity of our emotional pain are probably what activate defenses over time. Witnessing the suffering of children taxes any and all tolerance we may have to endure the pain of others. I believe that Jack and I did a lot of compartmentalization to cope with the changing situations during the course of Aimee's disease. We were too busy living through these events and trying to meet our family's needs to examine how defenses might have been working in our lives. At this point, I appreciate compartmentalization as part of how we survived. Maybe our daughters did something analogous in their childhood worlds.

For all of its virtues, there were ways that compartmentalization did not work for us. It facilitated pushing aside the ultimate questions raised by the disease, making it difficult to talk about Aimee's illness when we were relaxed at home after a difficult time in the hospital. The topic of death, once spoken as a word and topic, would destroy all illusions of normalcy and call for massive rearrangements of the file cabinet. I wondered what price we had paid for the protection of compartmentalization. Did it steal something from us?

Another possibility is that compartmentalization was the best we could have hoped for, a gift of precious value that helped us endure one of the most challenging situations in life reasonably well. Perhaps it should not be questioned, manipulated or replaced but rather regarded with gratitude and amazement as a form of human adaptation.

Our pilgrimage gave me a grander picture of what had happened over the years. It came at a time when compartmentalizing information about Aimee's disease was no longer necessary for me. My task upon return was not to protect myself from feelings but rather to get more in touch with them as my undefended, vulnerable heart continued to renegotiate home.

From Shadow to Light

To acknowledge and then own one's shadow is to admit there are many more sides to us that the world generally does not see. . . . Wherever we find ourselves, we need to honor the part of life that lies in shadow, to redeem those qualities we have forgotten or ignored.

Robert A. Johnson, *Owning Your Own Shadow*

I have learned things in the dark that I could never have learned in the light, things that have saved my life over and over again, so that there is really only one logical conclusion. I need darkness as much as I need light.

Barbara Brown Taylor, *Learning to Walk in the Dark*

One does not become enlightened by imagining figures of light, but by making the darkness conscious. The latter procedure, however, is disagreeable and therefore not popular.

Carl Gustav Jung, *The Collected Works of C.G. Jung*

Heart Work

Back home, I continued to ponder the potential for finding light in the dark. I'd always preferred the light—beautiful light. As an adult, Molly was much more willing to look at the darkness than I was. She had to take me by the hand and lead me to this place I so feared and disliked. Earlier, at times when life had taken me to the darkness, it felt malicious, not-me, an improper place to be. In this later darkness with my family, I finally found its energy and growth—its light. Could I continue to build up enough tolerance for my uncomfortable feelings to see more of the dark's treasures? What else could I learn about the shadow parts of myself?

We all have a shadow according to Jung, the disowned parts of ourselves, some negative and others unacknowledged gold. An analyst described it for me as follows: The shadow can come in times of uncertainty, doubt, ambiguity, growth, even creativity. . . .The shadow is all that I am, but am unaware of, at any given time. What unconsciously hides in that dark depends upon our early conditioning, personality development, and our ideas about how we want to present ourselves to the world. Getting to know our shadow helps us to see our true humanity which includes parts of ourselves that have been hidden and unacknowledged. They can become best friends offering us answers and insights that we didn't have earlier.[13]

The whole process of our family toiling together in such a complicated and intensive manner challenged our defenses, the ways we each used to protect ourselves from psychological pain. It increased the likelihood that we would do or say things that we normally wouldn't, that our shadows would have an opportunity for expression. Unconsciously, Molly had primed us to hear from our shadows by the very nature of the work she had proposed.

One of her greatest gifts to me during our family work was the challenge to develop a more intimate relationship with my anger. At times she directly tried to get me in touch with it—"You have to be so angry about Aimee's death, Mom"—hoping that I would express it, she could witness it, and then feel more comfortable to express her own. However, my anger stubbornly hid out in the darkness of my shadow,

Returning with the Questions

biding its time, protecting me, but also depriving me of a broader and more inclusive sense of who I am.

As our work together progressed, anger gradually came out in unplanned exchanges—an emotional rehashing of an episode from shortly before Molly left for college; uncomfortable confrontations during the Christmas holidays; a screaming rage from me based upon misinformation from a therapy session. Molly seemed willing to listen to my wrath in any form.

Accessing and expressing my anger about Aimee's death was far more difficult.

When I thought back to the time of Aimee's diagnosis, I couldn't remember thinking that a non-benevolent, vindictive God was testing me in some way, or that I had done something horrible that caused my daughter's illness, or that we had been singled out for this challenge. Like Rabbi Harold Kushner whose son had died of a rare disease in his early teens, I accepted that there is randomness in the universe, a philosophical idea key to his book *When Bad Things Happen to Good People* which I read in tandem with the early days of Aimee's chemotherapy.[14]

In general I didn't see frequent expressions of anger as helpful in raising children. After leukemia, this belief was even more powerful for me as I looked at my ill daughter and the rest of our family. Did I exile my anger to some dark part of my unconscious so that it wouldn't interfere? Did I do a kind of spiritual bypass of anger, thinking that I was too good to feel that way? Did it join in with my other painful emotions to create those discomforting facial expressions that my daughter described? Or did I simply not feel this emotion? I am not sure of the answers to these questions.

While in the Wilderness of telephone talks with Molly, months of reading the diaries, listening to our talks with Dr. Provisor, and considering Christmases over time, my anger about Aimee's death began to emerge from my shadow. At a purely visceral level, I experienced my anger that she had suffered so much both physically and emotionally; that she was not alive to be with us in our joys and sorrows; that she did not get to grow up and use her talents as an adult; that we didn't have the pleasure and satisfaction of watching her evolve as a person; that I don't get to see my daughters interact, have fun and even occasional conflict as adults; that Aimee and Molly didn't get to challenge, question and laugh with each other for many more years; that we don't have Aimee at our family get-togethers; that my daughters no longer get to plan, collaborate, and create together; that Aimee's absence deeply affected her sister's development; that Molly didn't get to have her sister here at times when she needed her, and that she will not have a sibling by her side when Jack and I die.

Out of the Wilderness and back home, I continue to become more intimate with my anger. This effort works best in small doses and recognitions. I don't dwell on it, nor do I ignore it. Jack patiently listens to my anger expression and later analysis, more of his gifts to me. It remains consciously off limits in many places and relationships in my life; I'm comfortable with these restrictions. I write and draw about anger in my journal usually in reds, oranges, yellows, often in fire-like strokes with slight hints of blue. It fades, reappears at expected and unexpected times. I once again examine it in its current time and place. I am getting better at accepting it, figuring it out, doing no harm. Sometimes I find water to put around the flames for containment. Sometimes I can't. I'm getting to know these times better.

I have read numerous books about anger. They have been helpful, but none of them have fully spoken to me. Repressing and expressing anger both have their negatives. Changing thoughts as an approach to anger reduction is disrespectful to its richness. Labeling anger as simply a surface emotion for other emotions feels too generalized. Miriam Greenspan, whose book *Healing through the Dark Emotions* has been a great comfort to me, described anger as an "honorable emotion—as long as we don't use it as a fuel for hatred and violence," one that required another whole book of its own.[15] Her acknowledgement of the complexity of anger as an emotion was reassuring to me.

Ironically, simple advice and activities have been most helpful to me. The Vietnamese Buddhist monk Thich Nhat Hanh wrote about the wisdom of acknowledging anger within, taking good care of it, and ultimately accepting mud as part of the growing lotus.[16] Molly encourages me to be in touch with my anger and to see it as a normal part of life. I witness it, and then go color, paint, glue, talk and cry. As time goes on, I feel more appreciative of the ways anger informs my life, and myself about myself. I've decided that this process will traverse time and require mindfulness, self-awareness, and patience as well as respect for the emotion's message.

I am amazed at the power and energy of this dark emotion but have become less intimidated by these characteristics. Sometimes I even enjoy them. I embrace the words of the poet David Whyte: "But anger truly felt at its center is the essential living flame of being fully alive and fully here; it is a quality to be followed to its source, to be prized, to be tended, and an invitation to finding a way to bring that source fully into the world through making the mind clearer and more generous, the heart more compassionate and the body larger and strong enough to hold it."[17]

For all the ways that I work on it psychologically, physically and spiritually, a residue of anger remains over the fact that Aimee is dead. I don't go around feeling this way most of the time, but holidays, birthdays and anniversaries often create frightening mixtures of emotions in me.

My anger tells me how deeply I loved Aimee and how heartbreaking it is not to have her physically with us. Mostly it is Aimee's presence and essence that I miss, my first born, the strong life force that finally made me a mother in my mid-thirties and graced our family with her presence over the years. Both love and anger power my writing and my commitment to both preserve Aimee's memory and honor Molly's struggle. As part of my relationship and contract with anger, I ask it to continue transforming me.

The more I have expressed my own anger, the less angry Jack has become. Many of us who are uncomfortable with anger have partners who are willing to express it, often for both of us. Jack had often carried this burden. He seemed relieved to loosen up in this unconscious role. In the later years of our pilgrimage, he became the calmer partner many days. Space opened up for him to claim and express more of his sensitivity and humor at home and beyond.

As anger and I understood each other better, more unacknowledged parts of myself leaked, sometimes splashed, out of me. I couldn't seem to stop their intrusion—the Anti-Intellectual, the Sarcastic, the Talkative, the Confident, the Intellectual. They expressed themselves after years of crowded, cramped conditions in my unconscious, *so* uncomfortable that their manifestation felt like a calculated revolution on their part. Sometimes they arrived with a sense of grace and at others with an awkwardness that created 3 a.m. wakeups full of self-questioning. Have I offended people? Am I making any sense? Is this all just within me and nobody else really notices or senses it? This involuntary release of more of who I am was uncomfortable as well as exhilarating. What are these gifts from the shadow asking of me? How am I to act upon them and integrate them into my life? How can I get comfortable with the gold? Can I count on this awareness and energy to continue?

The more I have been able to accept parts of my shadow, the more I have been able to see my true humanness. I've begun to allow imperfection her fair share in my life after a carefully considered swap of perfectionism for wholeness. I have started to own my ability to express myself and to ask reasonable questions. I've welcomed enhanced creativity into my life with open arms. I am learning to live with and cherish the joy, discomfort, and even the vulnerability of this evolving state. An additional gift is increasing compassion, tolerance and acceptance of other people's darkness.

As Miriam Greenspan wrote, "When we listen closely to what hurts, we learn what life is asking of us."[18] Over time, I've concluded that life wants from me exactly what Molly wanted of me—to be authentically who I am.

"Calm down, Mary Jane. Be who you are." With virtually no coaching, that is what Jack often says to me, exactly what I need to hear, an echo of his daughter's wish, and my own wish for myself.

Relationships in our Family

> *What vulnerability asks of us, ultimately, is not control of our emotions but transformation of our consciousness through emotional openness.*
>
> *If we can hang in, and maintain our openness to grief, we find that the ego reestablishes itself with an expanded vista: less isolated and bound up in its narcissistic shell, more open and compassionate, and free of compulsive maneuvers to avoid pain, more connected to spirit. . . . In a sense, grief is a birth process from ego to spirit.*
>
> Miriam Greenspan, *Healing through the Dark Emotions*

So much in life flows from the ongoing nature and state of our close relationships. The most frequent question that I was asked after Molly returned to New York in 2010 was, "How did this therapy and filming experience affect your relationship with Molly?" I was sure that something profound and extraordinary had happened. As I continued to ponder this question, I wanted to include my relationships with Jack and Aimee, as well as mine with myself. I knew that any answers were open-ended, subject to change and perhaps new questions.

Our pilgrimage, by its very nature, was a time of vulnerability. We were held together with a schedule, a caring and compassionate therapist, Molly's cameras, and our home where we had lived with Aimee. Simultaneously, the situation had an edge to it that took us out of our comfort zones and to places where growth and creativity were possible. As we worked together intensively and became more real to each other, we shed some of the ways we had protected ourselves. Much like a snake molting an outgrown skin, each of us became more vulnerable. Out of this experience, our relationships were transformed.

Grief takes time and patience. It is gruelingly hard work that could make a person want to 'get over it' quickly and exclude other people who might enhance the process. I knew that I needed Molly, Jack and Aimee to expand and enrich this lifelong process for me.

Realizations came out of our pilgrimage that helped me to see Molly in ways I hadn't been able to earlier. We learned that we had misinterpreted and misunderstood some of each other's behaviors. A simple example is my equating adult Molly's occasional lack of comments in a family situation to her simply not noticing or caring about what was going on. I came to realize that she *was* noticing, just not commenting. She had practiced this behavior for years in the shadow of her sister's illness. It had been a difficult behavior to shake in adulthood. I still want more verbal expression from her sometimes. When I ask for clarifications and expansions, the words flow from her. Often asking is unnecessary.

I came to recognize a certain awkwardness across the years in bringing our younger daughter center stage in our rearranged family, probably tied to the years when she was "the wind beneath my wings" for Aimee. The discomfort was for Jack and me, Molly, and, dare I say, the village surrounding us. An alteration of perspective, an energy reshuffle, and an embrace of the new configuration. These initially uneasy adjustments have evolved into a gracefulness in recent years.

I started to understand the accumulation of Molly's feelings, possibly from as far back as her sister's diagnosis. She had gone forward with a mass of emotions, further complicated by the death of her sister, the person Molly would have relied upon to help her through such confusion. There hadn't been two separate reservoirs of emotion, before death and after death, but rather a developmental band of feelings across very formative years in her life. I wondered how the death itself and this continuum of feelings fit together. A complicated question to ponder.

When she visited us in 2011, Molly said that I had changed. I asked her how I had changed. She answered, "You're more socially connected, more relaxed, more present, and more intellectually curious." I asked her, "Than when?" She answered, "When I was a kid growing up." After a pause, she added, "When I lived here." Had we each changed that much or were we seeing each other differently?

Molly and I have a closer and more relaxed relationship. I respect her perspective. I feel deep compassion for her. We continue to take risks in our communication and laugh together more. She is an independent person but shares her life with us. I'm expressing more of myself as I get to know myself better. I've learned to live with that bit of anxiety I feel when I press 'send' for a particularly expressive email I've just written. Her response is inevitably positive or humorous.

We have outgrown the former version of our relationship.

At this point, I consider Molly my *kalyana-mitra*, a concept of friendship from the Buddhist tradition which means *noble friend*.[19] Such a friend does not accept pretense. Instead she gently and firmly confronts her friend's blindness. My noble friend helped me to see what I was unable to see for myself. We have worked long and hard to be able to navigate uncomfortable and awkward terrains as mother and daughter. I treasure and respect us.

Molly is the one who will live the longest with our loss of Aimee. It is siblings, not parents, who carry the loss of a child for the longest time, spanning developmental stages and major life events.

Jack and I both readily said *yes* to Molly's wish to come home and talk about Aimee's death. We both suspected that her recollections would be different than ours, just as ours were often different from each other's. What we didn't anticipate was the positive impact that this experience would have on our relationship with each other.

In therapy, I witnessed Jack's vulnerability, the effort he made to express his feelings, how much he loved and missed Aimee, his wish to be closer to Molly, his love and concern for her. He cried more than I had ever seen him cry. Later I saw Jack do all he could to help Molly and me with our creative projects, whether a task required a few mouse clicks or days of effort. He answered our calls and emails with solutions, specifics, and alternative suggestions. His efforts seemed motivated by the new energy in our family rather than his own need for closure.

Jack and I became closer through this whole process. We were the parents. Neither of us felt singled out by Molly nor was she simply viewing us as a unit. We were in this together and as individuals. It had taken both of us to raise the girls, each contributing in our unique ways. How many fathers read the classics out loud to their daughters, take two children to the grocery store each week, and write dates on their daughters' art work? We felt yoked together in this labor of understanding our daughter who had come to us with her arms extended and saying words that were difficult to hear.

In addition to listening to Molly, we found ourselves listening to each other more carefully. We sought each other out with our uncomfortable emotions and questions. We consulted and reflected. We worked at speaking our truth to each other—good practice for speaking it to our daughter. The whole project drew us together, not in a circling wagons kind of way, but more in a sense of cooperation and curiosity.

And then I saw Jack begin his own creative project, later in the process than Molly and I. It is based upon his own talents, developed over his years of preparing PowerPoint presentations for class lectures. He began to scan or digitize all of our Aimee pictures from pregnancy on. As he went through her scrapbooks, he asked me numerous questions about dates and what was going on. In discussing these questions, we relived so many events together, sometimes grabbing one of the diaries to make sure we had the details right. We laughed and cried. He continued. He still continues. He is and always has been deeply appreciative that he is the father of Aimee and Molly, attesting to that experience as the most important in his life. We feel a deep sense of sharing this journey, of having gone through life together with all its ups and downs.

How has my relationship with Aimee changed? She feels like a comfortable part of daily life to me, like she's consistently here in some way. Sometimes I'm reminded of pregnancy—that life within that I knew was there but could not see. Our house, so many years later, looks different than it did when she was alive, but I feel her presence in this redefined space, not just physically and spiritually but also psychologically. I have come to know her better. I feel like we know each other better.

I see Aimee in a more complicated way through Molly's vision of her. I have a richer appreciation for her role as a sister—how much she shaped her sister's view of herself and how deeply the girls were connected as human beings. I feel gratitude for the ways she mentored her sister and supplemented our parenting. I believe that the girls were truly *anam cara*, a Celtic term for soul friends who share a relationship of trust and openness, an eternal connection.[20]

What was it like to be Aimee living with all of her talent and creative ability, paired with an increasing sense that the length of her life was limited? How did that affect what she did on a daily basis? And what was it like being an equally talented younger sister watching Aimee in a possibly altered state of cognitive and creative output? What did each of the girls think and feel about the complexity of their lives as children that they were unable to express in words?

I comprehend Aimee's life at a deeper level, how her relationship with her disease changed over the years, how she used her creative energy in evolving forms over time. I've always admired her deeply, but I see her more clearly—how her beautiful mind, her kindness, her generosity helped to maintain strong relationships that remained with her to death.

While I was reading the diaries, I felt my sadness and anguish about her disease at an even deeper level than I did when she was alive. I saw her humanness more clearly—her anger, confusion, and utter sadness about this disease that was killing her. As I became more open, I was able to connect with her expressiveness. On the pages, I found her to be more accessible and communicative than I had remembered her. Another relationship in my life functioning more comfortably.

Aimee dwells with us in a less agitated way than she did during those last years of intense suffering. She feels more grown up to me. I know that she has knowledge that I don't have. Talking to her is more relaxed, spontaneous and frequent—any time from when I look at her portrait hanging along our stairway or light a candle before I sit down to write. I can look at pictures and video of Aimee or listen to tape recordings of her reciting nursery rhymes without immediately exiting the room in tears. I don't have many dreams of her, but nearly always when I do, she simply walks into our home or backyard and, without a whole lot of fanfare, resumes her life with us. I find those dreams comforting. I welcome Aimee walking into our lives—any time.

My relationship with myself has changed. Most of my life, I have felt uncomfortable talking about myself. I was conditioned as a child to avoid such "self-centered" behavior and instead to get other people to talk about themselves, great training for my later career as a psychotherapist. I talked enough to do well in school, to always have friends, and to succeed professionally. For years I had all sorts of thoughts and observations that were difficult for me to express because I thought they were incorrect, uninteresting, or probably simpleminded. At some point, I knew that they were actually pretty complicated but would require me to talk too much trying to explain them and what if I couldn't?

Having children and later dealing with Aimee's leukemia really got me talking. If I didn't ask, articulate, and think out loud, the questions wouldn't get asked or answered. Molly's proposal and all that ensued from our family's pilgrimage took talking to a whole new level for me. The situation created a release of so many words that I was concerned about being hyper-verbal sometimes. Verbal containment became a new effort for me. Talking is much more spontaneous now, and I abstain from obsessing later about something I've said. The discomfort is there, but it is toughening me up in my efforts to express myself. Jack and I talk more than ever and take unabashed pleasure in this pursuit. He said he has never heard this level of verbal expression about what I'm thinking. He likes it.

I experienced a sense of surrender in our work and shared my more human side without even meaning to—the not-so-perfect, not-so-composed, not-so-nice Mary Jane. In being more fully myself, I gave my daughter permission to be herself, or maybe it was vice versa. I started grieving for myself in a more primal and communal way—in wails and sobs and words. When I began to write, I learned that I was an historian, a recorder of data. I felt enriched by adding that descriptor to my sense of self.

I am less concerned with impressing people and more concerned about being an authentic human being. I do more of what I want and care less about what people think of me. I am deliberate about how I spend my days and feel very protective of my time and energy. I trust my thought processes and verbalize them frequently. I feel smarter, more confident, more grounded. Decisions get made more easily. I am

Returning with the Questions

more willing to make commitments; I am more willing *not* to make commitments. I nurture my creativity and use the arts to sustain myself. I don't wear make-up as often. I am highly likely to follow my intuitions. Every day I take some risk in communication and tolerate the uncomfortable feelings that come up. The discomfort is waning.

In the big picture, I feel like I have both of my girls back, and in some relearned sense, our family back. And myself.

Back at home, my questions about relationships in our family are quite general. How will all these interpersonal shifts evolve over time? How can we continue to keep the energy of our pilgrimage alive? How can we best handle the times when we regress to old ways of behaving that we thought were gone?

I relax into these questions by calling to mind a vivid and comforting image of our family, one that really happened but was not filmed or photographed. The three of us are sitting together on our therapist's couch—our arms around each other, Molly between Jack and me—at the end of a single therapy session nearly two years after we had finished our original work. We are all smiling with tears flowing down our cheeks, feeling close to each other with a full sense of Aimee's presence surrounding us. This tableau captures what we had grown into as a family. When I reflect on this scene, I feel only love. Our family ready to evolve wherever our extraordinary time together guides us.

Epilogue

I finished the first draft of this book before watching my daughter's film *Peanut Gallery*, three weeks before its premier at the Indianapolis Film Festival in July of 2015. During the time of cameras in our lives almost five years earlier, we had little sense of where our work together was going and what, if anything, would happen to this footage. We thought of the camera as an important element in helping Molly to feel safe during our therapeutic efforts. We did not think of ourselves as making a movie. About 150 hours of footage sat for over two years before Molly looked at it and then decided to make a film. She invited us many times to see the editing as it progressed. I had already begun writing this book by then and did not want to be influenced by Molly's telling of the story. Jack also declined over concerns that seeing various versions of the film would destroy his objectivity in watching the finished project. Molly was adamant that we needed to see *Peanut Gallery* before we went to the premiere. She knew that watching this footage would be a deeply emotional and challenging experience for us, and she was right. Jack and I viewed it together at home and followed up with a prearranged telephone processing session with Molly immediately afterwards.

Peanut Gallery and *Heart Work* tell the story of events we lived through from different points of view and developmental perspectives. The book covers a wider swath of time and took a longer time to create, but both are examples of perceptions shaped by age, relationship, role, personality, generation, and life experience. I hope that the film and book can be used together in some teaching situations. To me, they are each a tale of the healing power of love, honesty, commitment, communication, and the creative process.

Our family debated about divulging this story. We understood clearly that it was a choice on our part. An inexorable energy was pushing us forward, but it was accompanied by an uncomfortable anxiety about exposing some of the best and worst of ourselves. At the same time, we felt a connection with and obligation to our fellow travelers—grieving siblings, ill siblings, parents, relatives, friends, nurses, physicians, therapists, researchers, caring bystanders, and others

Heart Work

who grieve. Over time, we concluded that the possibility of broadening the conversation on sibling grief and family relationships after loss was worth the risk of possible accusations of narcissism or naïveté. We decided that the benefits outweighed the risks and strongly intuited that this was not just our story.

I believe more and more that young siblings grieve across time in ways that are meshed with their developmental tasks, cognitive and emotional maturity, and the complexity of their relationship with the deceased sister or brother. As parents, we sustain and nurture grieving siblings the best we can across the years. For Jack and me, Molly became an adult when we were all able to communicate at a much deeper level about her sister's illness and death. A convergence of life experiences nudged her in that direction at the same time as we were moving into new phases of adult maturity in our own lives. I'm not sure that we could have done this work earlier or if it would have been as effective if we had. There is no formula for when ideal concurrences may happen in life. Openness to their possibility seems like the critical factor to me.

Helping grieving siblings is one more task that parents, who have lost a child and have other children, are challenged to undertake. The potential for parents and families to enrich their own growth through this process seems enormous to us.

We started out hoping to assist Molly with her sibling grief within the context of the three of us. The unexpected gift was how powerfully Aimee returned to her sister's life and back into our family. Looking at pictures, sharing memories and perceptions, crying together, challenging each other, disclosing our dreams about Aimee, listening, questioning, taking risks, using the camera as witness—some synergy among all of these activities during our time together brought Aimee back into our family. All of our relationships, including ours with her, need to be nurtured in ways we keep discovering—sometimes awkward, challenging, heartbreaking, sentimental—all born of a new respect and understanding that sustains us as our family moves forward.

The Irish philosopher and poet, John O'Donohue, suggested that perhaps death isn't such a big deal to the dead.[1] He wondered how they

Epilogue

look at us scampering around on this planet, seeking to be special or famous or just to get through the day intact. It is all so short, over so quickly. We spend the first half seeking so much and, if we are fortunate, the later years focusing on what is most important. Yes, the dead must wonder about us and yet simultaneously know something about this process called life, having lived some version of its infinite possibilities.

    I find it comforting to think that death may not be such a big deal and that maybe it won't be cataclysmic when it happens. Maybe Aimee has total perspective on her life, what it was about, where she impacted humans, how much we loved her, how much we tried—as humanly flawed as it may have been. Maybe she is mildly entertained by all this writing about grief and death, all the anguish and tears. She may have that sweet, knowing smile on her face at this moment. Maybe she doesn't even think of Molly as alone at all, for she is always with her.

Gratitudes

I feel so much gratitude toward the people who have helped me to write this book.

I am very indebted to all the researchers and writers who have paved the way for an expanded look at sibling grief. I want to thank a few in particular. I am very grateful to Elizabeth DeVita-Raeburn whose book *The Empty Room: Understanding Sibling Loss* was my awakening to all that I didn't know about this topic and my surviving daughter.[1] I read it, handed it to Jack, and immediately sent a copy to Molly. It elevated our family to a level of consciousness that enabled us to begin our therapeutic venture. Betty Davies' *Shadows in the Sun: The Experiences of Sibling Bereavement in Childhood* provided the research and overview that I was craving.[2] I read this groundbreaking book with a fervor I usually reserve for my book club's latest find. Reading Helen Rosen's *Unspoken Grief: Coping with Childhood Sibling Loss* was like listening to a wise and learned aunt who knew a lot about a topic that I wanted to understand better.[3] Victor Cicirelli's *Sibling Relationships across the Life Span* provided substantive background on sibling relationships.[4] Dr. Cicirelli has been at Purdue University for as long as I can remember. He kindly met with me early in my writing and asked all the important questions.

I feel deep gratitude for my writing group, Astrid Hastak and Lisa Lee Peterson, who have been my most long-standing, loyal, and helpful writing companions over time. I was inspired and nurtured by attending writing retreats with Bloomington's Women Writing for (a) Change and workshops at the Indiana Writers Center in Indianapolis. My spiritual director, Laurel Simon, recently deceased and greatly missed, was my faithful mentor in the discovery and cultivation of my creative energy. Warren Sibilla and Donna Flanagan, both Jungian analysts, helped me to deepen my thinking in ways that would have escaped me without their insights. Presenting a personal story session at the Association for Death Education and Counseling (ADEC) annual meeting in 2014 gave me a sense of community that energized my writing. Kim Evans provided very insightful feedback on my first draft and helped me to embrace my role as a storyteller.

Thanks to Dr. Arthur Provisor, now retired, who responded to my efforts to contact him so many years after his intense eight years with Aimee and our family. His willingness to read and give permission for the subchapter based upon taped conversations in his office says so much about the humanity and generosity of this physician.

Jack and I both have wonderful siblings with families who have always been with us in the kindest and most loving ways. They somehow found a balance between encouraging me to write this book and not asking me too often when it might be done.

My friends, close by and far away, found that same balance and supported me in ways spoken and unspoken that I deeply appreciated.

Most importantly, thanks to my family. I could not have written this book without my husband Jack. When I started to write, he methodically updated my computer equipment and answered my daily questions. Frequent reminders to "back up" were annoying but appreciated. He tracked down virtually any book or article I had difficulty finding. He patiently provided helpful feedback on my manuscript when I asked for it. Nor could I have written it without my daughter Molly. She helped me through some ups and downs in the writing process with patience, calm, and solid advice. Her feedback on my almost finished manuscript was encouraging, thought provoking and challenging. Her notations about what was touching or revelatory to her were very meaningful to me. Aimee was very present through it all, an approving energy, nudging me a bit at times, as she did when she was alive.

Mary Jane Gandour, PhD
West Lafayette, Indiana

Notes

Prologue

1. Sarah York, *Pilgrim Heart: The Inner Journey Home* (San Francisco: Jossey-Bass, 2001), 8-13. These pages contain a detailed description of the four phases of pilgrimage.

Chapter One ~ *Venturing into the Unknown*

1. *Biographical Note:* Our family lived in West Lafayette, Indiana, a university town of about 30,000 where Purdue University is located. My husband Jack was a professor at the university, a former Peace Corps volunteer in Thailand, later a theoretical linguist turned cognitive neuroscientist. I had taught secondary school for ten years before becoming a clinical psychologist. Professionally this place was very good to both of us. Although we had not set out to live in the Midwest, we grew to love our new geographical home, particularly after our daughters were born—Aimee in 1979 about two years after our arrival here and Molly almost four years later in 1983. The girls went to school in this community where education is deeply valued and supported in the public schools. Even as young children, they seemed to thrive on all the opportunities available here in the middle of the cornfields.

Chapter Four ~ *Returning with the Questions*

1. Sarah York, *Pilgrim Heart: The Inner Journey Home* (San Francisco: Jossey-Bass, 2001), 149, 171.

2. Trent Gillis, "To Hold Contradiction in Our Hands Is What Makes Us Unique as Humans (Video)," E-newsletter. *On Being* (onbeing.org). October 8, 2010.

3. Jeffrey C. Miller, *The Transcendent Function: Jung's Model of Psychological Growth through Dialogue with the Unconscious* (Albany: State University of New York, 2004), xi.

4. Louise DeSalvo, *Writing as a way of Healing* (Boston: Beacon Press, 1999), 62-66, 122-123. This book introduced me to the winner of the 1994 Nobel Prize for Literature, Kenzaburo Oe. In 1995

he wrote a non-fiction work about his handicapped son's survival through courage, creativity and the healing power of his family, *A Healing Family*, trans. by Stephen Snyder (New York: Kodansha, 1995).

5. Miriam Greenspan, *Healing through the Dark Emotions: The Wisdom of Grief, Fear, and Despair* (Boston: Shambhala Publications, Inc., 2003), 286-287.

6. Sherwin B. Nuland, *How We Die: Reflections on Life's Final Chapter* (New York: Vintage Books, 1995), 242.

7. *Consider the Conversation* is a series of PBS films created by two filmmakers who lost loved ones to severe chronic diseases. Their goal is to "inspire culture change that results in end-of-life care that is more person-centered and less system-centered." http://www.considertheconversation.org/

8. Myra Bluebond-Langner, "Worlds of Dying Children and their Well Siblings," in *Children Mourning Mourning Children*, ed. Kenneth J. Doka (Washington, D.C.: Hospice Foundation of America, 1995), 124-125.

9. Therese A. Rando, *Treatment of Complicated Mourning* (Champaign, IL: Research Press, 1993), 508.

10. Myra Bluebond-Langner, *The Private Worlds of Dying Children* (Princeton, NJ: Princeton University Press, 1978), 9.

11. Myra Bluebond-Langner, *In the Shadow of Illness: Parents and Siblings of the Chronically Ill Child* (Princeton, NJ: Princeton University Press, 1996), 147.

12. Ibid., 148-156.

13. Warren Sibilla, PhD, Personal communication at group teaching/discussion during *The Shadow: The Mysterious Other*, a contemplative retreat at Gilchrist Retreat Center, Three Rivers, MI, October 25-28, 2012.

14. Harold Kushner, *When Bad Things Happen to Good People* (New York: Anchor, 2004, 1991), 46.

15. Greenspan, *Dark Emotions*, xiii.

16. Thich Nhat Hanh, *No Mud, No Lotus: The Art of Transforming Suffering* (Berkeley, CA: Parallax Press, 2014), 13.

Notes

17. David Whyte, *Consolations: The Solace, Nourishment and Underlying Meaning of Everyday Words* (Langley, Washington: Many Rivers Press, 2015), 15-16.

18. Greenspan, *Dark Emotions*, 16-17.

19. John O'Donohue, *Anam Cara: A Book of Celtic Wisdom* (New York: Cliff Street Books, 1997), 25.

20. Ibid., 13-14.

Epilogue

1. John O'Donohue, *Anam Cara: A Book of Celtic Wisdom* (New York: Cliff Street Books, 1997), 226.

Gratitudes

1. Elizabeth DeVita-Raeburn, *The Empty Room: Understanding Sibling Loss* (New York: Scribner, 2004).

2. Betty Davies, *Shadows in the Sun: The Experiences of Sibling Bereavement in Childhood* (Philadelphia: Brunner/Mazel, 1999).

3. Helen Rosen, *Unspoken Grief: Coping with Childhood Sibling Loss* (Massachusetts: Lexington Books, 1986).

4. Victor G. Cicirelli, *Sibling Relationships Across the Life Span* (New York: Plenum Press, 1995).

Appendix A

Timeline of our Family's Grief Work

2009
Oct 19 Molly proposes family work on Aimee's death.

2010
Apr 18 Molly arrives by train; we began our therapeutic work.
Jun 6 Molly returns to New York.
Nov 24 At Thanksgiving, we decide on more therapy over holidays.
Dec 20 Molly flies to Indiana for Christmas and more grief work.

2011
Jan 15 Molly returns to New York.
Jun 16–19 Molly and I do more talking and filming in NY.
Jul 6 I sort out the diaries I had kept on each of my daughters.
Sep 11 Molly and I start weekend telephone interviews.
Sep 20 I start to read and do some writing about the diaries.
Dec 25 Molly spends the holidays in New York.

2012
Jan 21 Molly and I finish our last telephone interview.
Apr 26 I finish my first reading of the diaries.
May (last week) Molly and I listen to/talk about the medical tapes.
May 28 Molly commits self to making a film about her sibling grief.
Jul 12 I locate and talk to Aimee's hematologist.
Dec 23–27 Molly spends holidays in West Lafayette.

2013 until the present. Our journey continues!!!

Appendix B

Timeline of Aimee's Illness

1986
Jan 22 Aimee is diagnosed with Acute Lymphoblastic Leukemia at Riley Children's Hospital in Indianapolis and hospitalized for ten days to begin chemotherapy.
Feb 5 Bone marrow in remission (day 14).

1988
Jul 22 Completion of treatment protocol begun at diagnosis.

1990
Jan 3 First relapse. Starts an intensified version of earlier treatment.
Jan 31 Bone marrow in remission (day 28).
Jun 3–5 Family visits the University of Minnesota Medical Center to investigate bone marrow transplant options for Aimee.

1992
Jul 13 End of treatment for first relapse. Bone marrow indicates a second relapse. Started Aggressive Relapse Protocol.
Oct 21 Bone marrow approximates remission (day 99).

1993
Feb 14 Potential unrelated bone marrow donor is found.
Mar 20 Potential donor refuses to participate farther.
Oct 12 Third relapse.
Oct 22–31 Investigational drug at University of Minnesota administered without success. Return home.
Dec 4–20 Develops pulmonary/pericardial aspergillus and pneumonia. Surgery to remove fluid from behind heart, home hospice care after.

1994
Jan 10 Miraculously achieves remission; later returns to school.
Feb 22 Fourth relapse, make plans for last possible chemotherapy.
Mar 20 Hospitalized with very high fever. In next days diagnosed with overwhelming sepsis and Acute Respiratory Heart Disease.
Mar 25 Moved to Pediatric ICU when she couldn't breathe.
Mar 26 Aimee died there at 5:35 p.m.

Appendices

Appendix C

TO – ANYONE – WHO – WANTS – TO – READ – IT

December 14, 1993

Dear Everyone at W.L.J.H.S.,

Hi! I know you're all wondering how I'm feeling and how I'm doing.

If you didn't notice, I was really weak at school before I left. This was because my leukemia and medicines were killing my good body cells, and my body could not fight infection very well. I wore myself out at school too much, and I got a fever. I came to the hospital with a temperature and a lot of pain in my lungs. They put me on antibiotics and morphine, and they tried to figure out what I had. They found out I had pneumonia, but they didn't know if it was from a bacteria or a fungus, so they started giving me all these medicines.

A day or two later, my pulse went up really high. They found out I had a lot of fluid around my heart. They tried to drain it with one procedure, but it didn't work. I then had to have surgery to drain the fluid (the pneumonia caused the fluid), and they put in a tube to drain any more fluid that might come. They also took a biopsy of my lung. The surgery was successful, and they found out from the lung biopsy that what caused my pneumonia was a fungus. They're giving me antifungal medicine.

Now I'm recovering from my surgery, and I'm on some medicines. I should be able to come home by Saturday, but I'll still be on lots of medicines at home, and it's not guaranteed my pneumonia will go away.

Thank you so much for all the cards and letters that you guys sent me. I really appreciate them, and they cheer me up a lot.

When I come back, I will not be strong enough to go to school. I'll be able to keep up with a class or two, but I won't actually be able to come to school because it tires me out too much. I will come in every once in a while at lunch time so I can see everyone, though. I miss you, and I miss W. L. Jr. High!

Sincerely,
Aimee Gandour

Appendix D

From Mary Jane's Journal – Six to Nine Months after Aimee's Death

September 26, 1994 (Aimee's 6-month death date)

It has been 6 months since you left us, Aimee, and it is only now that I am able to begin to put some of this into words, although words have swum in my head and come out of my mouth probably to a greater degree than on any topic in my life.

I felt more in touch with you today because I talked to Erin, Kuleni, and Liz, each of them. They along with your other friends had been to your grave, and for the first time in many months somehow felt together. Your spirit did the uniting, I believe. I think that people are just beginning to know that you have died, to really confront the fact that you are no longer dwelling in our midst.

I miss you each day of my life and want so to hear you, touch you, talk to you, smell you, eat with you, cry with you, pray with you, encourage you, comfort you, just look at you. I want you back as part of our family—the stabilizer, the one who always had the answer, the mover of events.

I need to write about the events surrounding your death, what happened in those days and hours before. I've replayed all of that time in my head so many times and yet have this morbid fear of ever forgetting it. I have some regrets (not many) and have this idea that if I can write them down, I will be able to let them go more easily. I do regret that we didn't video your funeral and take pictures at church; I'm not sure why we didn't have someone do that. Sometimes I wish we had had your funeral a day later, but I don't know how I could have borne to not see you for one minute longer than we were separated after your death. I wish we had stayed longer at your graveside and that we had invited more people to our home, and yet it seemed so right and perfect just the way it was that day. I wish I had gotten a temporary marker on your grave the day of the burial. Why did it take me until today to finally call and do something about that? Sometimes I think that maybe we should have gone to the Pediatric Intensive Care Unit sooner and maybe they could have sedated you more slowly, but then I think about missing that beautiful Thursday night of phone calls and basketball and reminiscing. In the end I think that I believe that it all went just as it was meant to go, that God was holding our hands and that it was all as natural as the rising of the sun and the birds in flight. I feel calmer when I think that way rather than enduring torment that is probably only of my own making. Dad is so much better at letting go of that sort of thing than I am.

I bought a tape with Bette Midler's "Wind Beneath My Wings" over the week-end and as part of my rituals for the day, I listened to it in the van on the way to work and home. Didn't you know you were my hero?

September 29, 1994

Yesterday I finally put a little marker on your grave that Soller-Baker gave me with your name, birth and death dates on it. Hard to know why it would ever take me that long to get that thought and follow through on it. It is funny though. As time goes on, I slowly feel some sort of freeing up of energy to do productive, concrete sorts of things that truly help and assist with grief. I remember feeling so bound up for so long. In my cocoon stage, I called it. In the days after you died, I remember the most glorious of spring sunshine streaming through our windows. I played with flowers from your funeral. I changed water, rearranged them, placed them all around the house although primarily in the living room and dining room. Each day we would take more of them over to your grave until finally they were all upon you. I saved the green plants and have nurtured them over these months. Somehow I don't think we have lost a one. Molly and Ebba pressed flowers from various arrangements. Your friends all have some of these. I listened to CDs almost constantly as I wrote the 308 thank you notes that it took to tell people how much all their help meant to us. I didn't listen to just anything. The music could have no words (except Latin or Italian) and I played over and over the Benedictine monks' Gregorian chants, David Lanz, Susan Chiarro, piano themes from Andrew Lloyd Webber,

Pavarotti-Domingo-Carreras. I would sit at the desk in your room (the largest desk in the house, you know) and write and write, struggle, compose, cry, obsess over cards and notes, rip up notes and start over sometimes. That went on for over 3 months. I really wanted it to be just as it was. I'm not sure that even Jack and Molly understood.

There were other ways of behaving. I could not go near or into a TCBY. We had gone so often in the course of your treatment that I had that lovely, cool way of refreshing ourselves so intertwined with my emotions and memories that I couldn't bear to be near the place. There were times when nothing else would appeal to you to put into your mouth because your mouth sores were so bad or your appetite so poor. I just can't remember a time when you said no to that particular treat. You even chose it for your birthday rather than a cake. Molly, on the other hand, was quite comfortable with maintaining our Sunday night trips to TCBY - for her, I think, a way of feeling close to you. It took me about seven weeks, but I was finally able to join in and now it seems like a way of remembering you. I also couldn't listen to any music on the radio that had words. I would listen to classical music only and that lasted months, perhaps four, well into the summer. Popular music was just too much of a painful reminder of you (not that you didn't like classical) because that was part of our routine in the car, one of your times to be in touch with it.

October 5, 1994

Somehow I have felt better the last few days. How better? Perhaps not as obsessed with painful thoughts about you, but feeling more peaceful about you inside. I think I have had a sense of peace all along, but there does seem to be some transformation going on. Sometimes I wonder if it doesn't have to do with where you are on your journey, if perhaps you are growing more and more peaceful with your new transformation. After all, leaving here couldn't have been an all-or-nothing thing. I don't think you could go from the very involved life you led, from all the connectedness you had created, to simply dwelling without all of it. Maybe you have hung around in ways we cannot understand or maybe some part of us went with you on your journey and you have finally reached a place where some others on that side of transformation are walking closer to you. I feel a greater peace, as I said, and wish that there was some way I could know how you feel or what you're experiencing at this time. When we do meet, I am going to want to get a few issues clarified: (1) How and exactly when did you get this horrible disease that killed you? I want God to help me know this in exquisite detail; (2) What would you have looked like at age 14 if you had never gotten leukemia? I remember so vividly how stunningly beautiful you were the summer before you were diagnosed. I remember particularly your rich beauty when we were in Thailand and you had not been on chemo for many, many months; (3) What did you experience as you died and did you hear our words, feel our touch? I know you did, but I want to know that from you.

    I felt you nudge me in bed as if you were standing by my side about three weeks ago. I know it was you. But you weren't there when I turned to you. I wonder if you were at some crossroads in your journey and checking in with me in some way.

    When we had lunch with Sue (one of the nurses with us as you were dying) down at Methodist the week before school opened, I was astounded to learn that she had just happened to come into the hospital around an hour before you died. She, of course, wasn't supposed to be at the hospital that Saturday as Sue never worked on the week-ends. She had been out on her property, some wooded land she purchased about 45 minutes from Indy, and had old muddy boots and dirty clothes on. She said something just told her to go to the hospital. Something just drew her there. She had not called to see how you were doing and did not know how close to death you were. She said she really winged it on all the rituals she went through with us after you died, and that we were such willing participants that she just kept going.

    I feel like we're moving into a time of the year that is going to be rough, that will be filled with memories of all your final stages of treatment. Most notably I'm starting to think about Minnesota. Purdue plays them next week-end, and it was just around this time last year that you had a major relapse after working so hard to stay in remission for so many months. Grandma Gandour was here from Florida, and she had gone down with us to meet Dr. Provisor and to support you before and after some drugs and a bone marrow aspiration that day. Molly stayed at school.

October 18, 1994

Yes, it was that day, October 12, 1993 when we found out that you had relapsed. The next day you, Dad and I went down for another one of our crossroads meetings with your doctor. No options but Ara-C, an investigational drug at the University of Minnesota, or nothing. What would Ara-C be like? Three kids had died, and the whole office was opposed, especially the nurses: "You are not going to do that to Aimee!" Doing nothing meant increasingly frequent transfusions and pain that would require pain medication as you moved closer to death.

Your grave looks good. Someone (my bet is on Bill Stillwell) put down sod, transplanted the dusty miller, and arranged the flowers on the cement base for your gravestone. It was so comforting to see, and the place looks so much better than it did. A Muslim professional colleague of mine was talking today about how the state of those left behind on earth affects the ability of our loved one to progress in his or her death journey. That makes so much sense to me. The idea is that spirits stay around to be with us, because the leaving and the journey have their own pain on the other side. To the degree that we are unable and unwilling to let go, our dear spirit is slowed down in the journeying process that takes place after death.

It was so good to get the ouija board message from my friend in Michigan. It told us that you were moving well and dancing in the light. Even Grandma Gandour found comfort in that message.

Molly and I went to Rumpza's yesterday to buy Halloween pumpkins, and there on that beautiful hillside full of pumpkins, sunlight and shadows dancing on them, a gentle autumn breeze blowing, we felt your spirit; you were there for sure. I felt tearful, sad and comforted simultaneously. Those early years of your life spoke to me in some mysterious way with a vivid image of one of my all-time favorite photographs—you as a two year old sitting on top of a huge pumpkin, smiling beautifully and obviously feeling very empowered in that time and place. It was four years after that, I think, that that your little sister Molly joined you for a new and even more joyful time on that very same hill. It was followed by some more precious years of Indiana autumn rituals. You loved it all. The celebrations and occasions of life meant so much to you.

I don't know why it is, Aimee, but I am feeling a bit better. I don't know if it is a temporary state that is going to give way to a worse and more devastating time of confronting your death or if I am truly moving on and finding new ways to relate to you. I truly feel your power in my life and feel very deeply that I am going to do something very meaningful with it. Please stay with me. Be with us in whatever ways you are able and still manage to find the fulfillment of your new life. I think that part of the responsibility is up to us, and we seek people, words, experiences, and insights to help us stay close to you. I love you so much and miss you so much. I want you back. How can you do that? Is there any way that you can come back to us? My tears are flowing as I ask you this question. Please come back in some way; let me feel you in some special way over and above what we have of you each day. I'm being selfish, I think, but honest, I suppose.

November 9, 1994 (Aimee's 15th Birthday)

To my dear sweet baby girl, Today is your 15th birthday. It rained the entire day, tears from heaven, I say. But why? Surely dancing in the light must be wonderful, but maybe you are still capable of weeping over the void we feel, the loss we all suffer in not having you with us. And maybe you are still capable of missing all of us for surely there was some part of the divine we all shared in living our lives together. The pull of death helps us to see the beauty in human beings more than any other situation on this planet, I think. Dad, Molly and I went to 11:30 Mass together. I had ordered a beautiful arrangement of pink and purple flowers at the Blossom Shop which Molly and I took to the cemetery. I think I was there three times today. I felt overwhelmingly anxious this morning to the point that I went down to Carol's just to sit and talk and get centered. Now, Mary Jane, get settled on when this bulb planting ceremony for your birthday will be. Have faith; the answers will come to you.

On days like this, the hurt and confusion about it all feel so overwhelming. I feel helpless like I did on the day you died, that same empty, scared, confused, insecure feeling. I haven't fought it. I also haven't put pressure on myself today to do anything but "grief work" and I deeply respect myself for that. I will always love you and feel you in my life. I know that when Dad and I were having such a difficult time last week, you were there with grace for us which somehow reconnected us in a new and powerful way.

January 20, 1995

Molly is upstairs cooking dinner which brings back memories of when you used to do that or when the two of you did it together. Cooking and baking, another form of creative expression for the two of you. I think every day of things I want to write but somehow just don't get them written. I want to tell about the wonderful celebration of your 15th birthday at Grand View Cemetery on Saturday, November 12. We invited friends to come and plant bulbs at your grave so that when the first anniversary of your death comes next spring, we will have the beauty of those flowers to remember you by and comfort ourselves with. I read about bulbs and fretted about where and how to plant them and what ways we could use to protect them from rodents. At some point I turned it over to you. The decisions came with great calm and simplicity - crocuses over your grave (they would come up and bloom before they started mowing the cemetery in the spring), daffodils on each side of your monument (a bright and cheerful testimony to you, to spring), and tulips in a patch we cleared across the road (out of the way but extending the sphere of beauty and you). Your friends all came as well as parents, siblings, neighbors, colleagues, teachers, counselors. Boys from your class each planted a pink tulip bulb. That same day Patti and I drove down to southern Indiana to posthumously accept your Young Hero's Award at the State Student Council Convention. We cried.

Finally your grave stone is up - a pinkish granite from Minnesota done by Bill Stillwell from Frankfort, Indiana. He used the exact calligraphy you so often wrote on notes and invitations and came up

Appendices

with a beautiful cross and dogwood motif across the top. We included a butterfly for transformation, musical clef for your love of music, the WL symbol for your school, and put the piano quote on the back. "Life is like a piano. What you get out of it depends on how you play it." It finally came to rest on your grave on January 10, 1995, a cold snowy day. I may be wrong, but I think that that was the date when one year ago you went into remission, baffling everyone, for that blessed period of grace we had before you died. You went back to school and participated quite fully right up to the strings orchestra contest trip you enjoyed so much that Friday night before your last admission to the hospital ever. And you and Erin made it to History Day with Molly. We are actually at this point relieved that you never underwent a bone marrow transplant, Aimee. You would have suffered so and maybe would have died without the remarkable aliveness you maintained until your death. I can't stand that you're not here, but I know that you came to the earth to do exactly what you did.

Appendix E

"Christmas Times"
By Molly R Gandour
May 1999, 9th grade, age 15

"Molly, Molly! Wake up!"

Aimee gently shook me and whispered urgently. I grunted, rolled over and tried to drown out the noise.

"C'mon, Molly! It's Christmas!"

My eyes blinked open. I rolled back around and saw Aimee, my sister, looking right back at me. She was four years older than me, so it was her job to always wake up first on Christmas.

Christmas! I could hardly believe it. It was finally here! All the waiting was finally over! Our wish lists to Santa Claus had seemed to be sent such a long time ago. I thought that Christmas would never actually come. December was definitely the longest month of the year.

I realized then that I had actually fallen asleep last night. I thought that I never would. And I hadn't heard any prancing and pawing on the rooftop, like Aimee and I promised each other we would listen for.

Dad, like every other year, had read us "Twas the Night before Christmas," the old fashioned version, before we were sent to bed in suspense. ("The sooner you get to bed, the sooner Santa Claus can come.") We had slept in my room together on my trundle bed just like we did every night before Christmas. We whispered, guessed our presents, and laughed, muffled by our pillows, into the night, until our hopes and anticipations carried us off to sleep. Visions of toys and candy (we didn't know what sugarplums were) danced in our heads.

But now it was finally morning. Big grins crept across our faces, and we giggled. Had Santa Claus come? What had he brought us? Did he get our note? Did he eat our cookies? Did he get us what we wanted? What if we didn't get this or that? What if he hadn't come at all? Had we been good?

We scampered across the hallway to my parent's room.

"Wake up!" we called. "It's CHRISTMAS!"

Appendices

They rolled over a few times, mumbled a few things about how we got earlier and earlier every year, and it was only seven a.m., and then told us to wait for them at the top of the stairs.

I have distinct memories of sitting at the top of my stairs on Christmas morning. At the base of them, to the left, is the living room, filled with all our presents. You can see the door from the top of the steps, but you can't see into the room at all, as hard as we would strain to look at it at every angle possible. Butterflies danced in my stomach as I sat there in my plaid flannel Christmas nightie. Aimee and I made last minute gift guesses. I tried with all my might not to bug my parents about hurrying up. They took so darn long to get out of bed.

Finally, they appeared behind us and declared with their parental power, "All right."

We were off. Aimee and I tore down the steps, our flannel nighties streaming behind us. We made the sharp left at the bottom of the stairs.

"He came!!!!" we exclaimed, our voicing echoing glee and ecstasy.

I made the turn and there before us was a pile of gifts for each of us, mine on the left, Aimee's on the right. We ran to our gifts and dropped to our knees to examine them more closely.

"Look!!!"
"Oh, my gosh!"
"Look, he ate all our cookies!"
"And Rudolph ate the carrot and, look, he left us a note!"
"We'll read it later. Presents now."
"What's this?"
"Cool!"
"Wow!"
"I was right, Aimee!"
"Well, me too."
"Neat!"
"Mom, look!"
"Oh, that's nice. What is it, honey?"
"Oh, this is just what I wanted!"

Heart Work

Every year Santa Claus got Aimee and me one big present each and lots of little presents. That year was the year of the animals. I got my first real pet that Christmas. My first grade teacher kept a teddy bear hamster in the room, and I desperately wanted one. Santa Claus brought me a hamster! He was a little tan ball of soft, silky fur, all rolled up in the comer of his cage. Aimee got fish, which I thought were much less exciting.

The rest of the morning was spent sorting through presents from Santa Claus, searching through stockings and putting my whole arm into it just to make sure that I didn't miss any important gifts, and then frantically tearing wrapping paper off of gifts from friends and relatives. The big gifts have always come from Uncle Ed and Aunt Laurie, who take holidays quite seriously. I always got something a little bizarre and offbeat from my Uncle Tom. That year was the year of the Chia Pet. I was thrilled. Presents from both grandparents were always good because they sent money and my mom bought things I wanted with it. It was usually cute clothes from Grandma and Papap (my Mom's parents) and doll clothes or a cool toy from Grandma Gandour. Pio and Anne always send pretty tree ornaments. The afternoon was spent unwrapping, exploring, investigating, playing, and deciding how much I liked every gift I'd been given, plus also looking at all of Aimee's presents. Our tree that we had spent so much time and energy picking out and decorating twinkled over us, with its old homemade angel at the top. Then we sat down and watched "How the Grinch Stole Christmas" and "Frosty the Snowman." It always overwhelmed me that so many people would care enough to send me presents. I would sit happily in our living room all day, content with all my new belongings surrounding me.

Later on, we had a delicious dinner cooked by Mom. I ate till I could hardly move and then I got one more helping of everything, just for good measure. It was a holiday, so I decided I might as well celebrate. And, besides, it was the only time all year that Mom fixed roast beef.

Then we went on our traditional drive around the city. I guess it started one year as a way to digest our dinner before dessert and see all the lights around the city. I can't remember a Christmas when we didn't go on our drive. We counted all the houses we drove by that had Christmas lights up. I think that was the year we set our all-time record that has never been touched: three-hundred-something houses.

We returned home to a heavenly traditional dessert of Haagen-Dazs vanilla ice cream with crushed candy canes on top and Christmas cookies from the annual cookie exchange. I, of course, once again ate till my stomach practically popped. All too soon, it was one last look at the presents, and Aimee and I were sent off to bed once again.

I fell asleep warm, safe, and comfortable in my bed. As my mind floated between consciousness and sub-consciousness, visions of little sparkling lights, food, and presents floated leisurely through my mind. I felt so satisfied and secure.

That was the Christmas of 1991; I was seven years old and in first grade. I'm not sure exactly who my good friends were at the time. But I still remember the magic of Christmas and how excited I was to see that hamster sitting there. Santa Claus was good to me that year. It's funny how we can mark time, our state of mind, and our former levels of maturity by holidays. Every year when Christmas rolls around, it's time to look back on all past Christmases and just remember. The story of my Christmases tells so much.

During Christmas 1992 I had chicken pox. Somehow, the one time in my life when I got chicken pox was destined to be at Christmas time. However, I nearly forgot about my sickness with all the excitement. I got an American Girl "Molly" doll that looked very similar to me. Aimee got a brand new, beautiful pink bike. That spring, I watched in awe as she took off down the road on her new two-wheeler, ten-speed bike. I was pretty proud of myself, though, for soon I was following along behind on her old two wheeler banana seat bike.

That year, I also found out the "truth" about Santa Claus. I had been hearing weird rumors at school, like people had seen their parents putting out their Christmas presents and such. I wanted to know once and for all who was right.

"Mom?" I asked. "Is there a Santa Claus?"

The question that every parent dreads. She took a deep breath.

"Let me read something to you, Molly."

Heart Work

I sat on Mom's lap, and she began reading me the famous letter, "Yes, Virginia, There Is a Santa Claus." I listened very carefully to all the big words. When she finished reading, I looked up at her quizzically.

"So, what does that mean, Mom?"

I hadn't really understood the point, hard as I tried. She explained to me then that there was no Santa Claus in the sense of a guy who wore a red suit and came down your chimney. I could've guessed that from all the things I'd heard at school. Then she told me that there was a Christmas Spirit that led people to give gifts and be giving around Christmas time. For the next few years, when people asked me if I believed in Santa Claus, I told them, no, not the person, but that there was a ghost who came and whispered in our parents' ears what presents to give us. I couldn't wait to be a parent so I could be visited by the Spirit of Christmas.

The Christmas of 1993 was harder to celebrate. My sister, Aimee, had been diagnosed with leukemia at the age of six. She had chemotherapy, and was better, but later relapsed. She had been pretty bad lately, especially around Christmas. Sometimes she would get fevers in the middle of the night and Mom would rush her down to Methodist Hospital in Indy. She would spend some weekends in the hospital, making jewelry and catching up on homework. Dad and I would go down and visit her some of the time. That December, Aimee had gone to the hospital in a fever. Dad and I had rushed to the hospital when we heard that she was having heart surgery and was in intensive care. She had miraculously used her strong will and perseverance and pulled through with a smile. That Christmas, she was on portable oxygen. I remember decorating the tree, and she had a container to pull around that carried oxygen for her to live. She spent that entire Christmas with oxygen tubes in her nose. At the time, it didn't seem like that big of a deal to me. I had lived with her sickness as long as I could recall. Looking back, though, it's amazing that she smiled, laughed, and acted as if it were just another Christmas. I hardly realized that anything was different, for her smile gave me courage.

When Christmas 1994 rolled around, it was even harder to celebrate. We had to celebrate it without Aimee who had died last

March. My Mom, who is a psychologist, says that holidays usually make people fall apart or pull themselves together. Holidays are so enveloped by memory and tradition. I think that Aimee not being there actually made Mom, Dad, and I pull together.

This first Christmas was definitely the hardest though. It was not the same to sleep by myself, wake up on my own, and run across the hall to tell my parents to get up all by myself. Instead of two piles of gifts from Santa Claus, there was only one. There were fewer presents under the tree, and we ate less food at dinner. When we went out to count lights, I had to count them all by myself and we inevitably didn't get as many houses. Two definitely makes everything more fun.

At Christmas 1998, I had lost my Uncle Tom, the one who gave me funky presents, and my grandpa, who I called Papap. Losing people makes you realize how much they really contribute to your life.

Now I'll jump up to present day. Just this past year, we bought an artificial tree to save ourselves the annual debates at Lutterloh's nursery. Dad still reads me "Twas the Night before Christmas," plus Mom reads "The Polar Express," and I read "How the Grinch Stole Christmas." Usually after watching a movie or Saturday Night Live, I head off to bed anticipating morning and wondering how I would fall asleep. "Santa Claus" still comes, although he is a little less subtle in his hinting on my getting to bed early. ("C'mon, Molly, you know I'm getting old, so if you expect me to stay up late enough to, uh, be, I mean see Santa Claus, you better head to bed right now.") I still get excited every time I wait at the top of the stairs for my parents to get ready, then go downstairs, turn that corner, and see my presents. And I still stick my whole arm into my stocking to make sure I haven't missed anything important. To my great disappointment, I'm learning the rule that the older you are, the fewer presents you get. My day is spent lounging around, listening to new CD's, and trying out new gifts. I even still watch "Frosty the Snowman," although the mean guy who wants his hat back doesn't terrify me like he used to. Now, I help Mom pick out recipes, and we cook a vegetarian Christmas dinner together: Then, we go on our annual drive to look at Christmas lights. By now, we've scoped out the best neighborhoods to see the most garish, tacky displays of neon carolers, Rudolph's, and elves. But we've never beat our record that we set that one year in the number of houses we saw. We also still have ice cream with candy cane on top for dessert, but now we usually buy Healthy Choice vanilla. And I still eat tons, although I try to control myself.

When you're little, Christmas is so magical. It is cloaked in the allure and mystery of Santa Claus, the North Pole, wish lists, songs, and lots of cookies. I hope that Christmas will always be magical for me. When I think of Christmas, I think of so many things. I think of the smell of Mom's classic ginger cookies that she makes for the cookie exchange every year and begging for dough out of the bowl. I think of waking up and, in a moment, realizing that it's Christmas.

To me, though, Christmas is like one of the presents I got when I was in kindergarten. It was a huge, red, soft, and furry bear. I loved it the moment I got it. I proudly paraded it around as the biggest bear in our class during our "Teddy Bear Parade." It was as tall as I was. I slept with it every night, snuggling with it. As I grew older, it didn't seem as big, because I kept growing. It began to get matted and slobbery, but I hated when my mom washed it. One day, I just decided not to sleep with it anymore, and I never did again. But I still kept it nearby and loved it. It is still in my room to this day. It reminds me of childhood and Christmas.

As much as we would like it to stay the same, our views of Christmas change with the years. Hard lessons must be learned: friends change, and people die. Yet every year, Christmas rolls around, full of cheer and giving, no matter what our lives are like. It doesn't skip anybody. It doesn't wait for good times or bad times. It just comes, regardless. Life is ever-changing, never stable, full of constant struggle and growth. But Christmases go on and keep us connected and grounded in our past. The magic of Christmas is that it is always there, a break from normal life, a time to just relax and give and receive. Christmas is a reminder that life goes on.

I Remember

I want you to know that I remember.
I remember you reading the classics to me.
I remember the crab apple tree.
I remember pitching the softball and shooting hoops.
I remember thrilling office chair rides.
I remember how I would make you "lay with me."
I remember frozen M&M's, MiDels, Oreos.
I remember Dandy Candy.
I remember the smells of Bangkok.
I remember making Tomanetti pizza.
I remember steaming muffins and sizzling woks.
I remember PayLess shopping trips.
I remember it all.
I remember crisp fall days of apple cider,
football games & the Purdue band,
and sun-speckled summer days of
frozen bananas, sprinklers and fireflies.
I remember tear-streaked hugs.
I remember Wacky Jacky & Molly Dolly.
I remember picking raspberries.
I remember seeing the U.S.A. in our green van.
I remember "give 'em a goose."
I remember dazzling shows and restaurants.
And I will always remember.

For Mom & Dad, Christmas 2001
I love you,
Molly

About the Author

Mary Jane Mulvey Gandour is the granddaughter of Irish immigrants and grew up in East Meadow, NY and Pittsburgh, PA. She has a BA in English (Wheeling Jesuit University), an MAT in secondary English teaching (University of Pittsburgh), and a PhD in Clinical Psychology (Purdue University). She taught secondary school in Pennsylvania, Japan, California, Thailand and New Jersey, before becoming a clinical psychologist and raising two daughters in the Midwest. She has traveled extensively in this country as well as overseas, particularly in Asia. Her husband Jackson is a Professor Emeritus at Purdue University.

About the Cover Images

The front cover images for *Heart Work* were reproduced from art work by Molly Gandour, *The Toy Symphony*, 1992 (left), and Aimee Gandour, *Fantasy Zoo,* 1990 (right). The mediums used in both pieces were black marker and tempera paint. Both were created within the time frame of Aimee's first relapse (see pages 49-59).

I feel deep gratitude to Kathy Trout who cultivated the creative energy of our daughters as their art teacher in elementary school. Both of these works were created in Mrs. Trout's classroom at Happy Hollow Elementary where the artistic expression of children was lovingly nurtured and deeply valued.

I am also grateful to Loren Olson and Jim Altepeter for their artistic and technical assistance. The cover design for my daughters' original art work was created by Rena Loro Aiken of Camera Outfitters in Lafayette, Indiana.

Made in the USA
Middletown, DE
12 April 2018